MILITARY GHOSTS

MILITARY GHOSTS

Alan C. Wood

AMBERLEY

Naval, Military, and Military Aviation Ghosts and Legends compiled by Alan C. Wood.
A Gazetteer Guide for Ghost Researchers and Others.

This book is intended as a Gazetteer Guide for those interested in the supernatural. Locations are all important to the seeker, and one of the best people to contact is the County, Town or City Tourism Officer, who will supply you with maps and accommodation information on request. As we live in a global village, I have included several ghost stories from other countries.

First published 2010

Amberley Publishing
Cirencester Road, Chalford,
Stroud, Gloucestershire, GL6 8PE

www.amberley-books.com

British Library Cataloguing in Publication Data.
A catalogue record for this book is available from the British Library.

ISBN 978-1-4456-0171-7

Typeset in 10.5pt on 13pt Sabon.
Typesetting and Origination by Amberley Publishing.
Printed in the UK.

CONTENTS

Introduction

Our ancient ancestors world-wide had a primal non-understanding of death. Their dead were buried with tools, clothing, food and sometimes servants, all of which they had in earthly life. The belief was that they would need these in an afterlife.

This practice developed into ancestor worship and a belief in an afterlife – such beliefs became common and integral to most religions, and carried the promise of eternal life or immortality. The knowledge that there was an afterlife removed the fear of death and gave reassurance and comfort to many that they would see their loved ones again.

There now being an assumed afterlife, it was natural for man to try and contact those who had departed from human life, and for the departed to try and contact those they had left behind in earthly life. However religion frowned on, and still does, contact with those who have passed away from earthly existence. Yet some religions have a ceremony of exorcism! A strange anomaly.

For hundreds of years, world-wide ghost sightings have been reported on land, sea and, even before the advent of aircraft, in the sky. Some ghosts gradually disappear with the passage of time; others linger.

Over the centuries, where men have fought and butchered each other in mortal combat, their ghosts, phantoms, or spirits are consistently reported re-fighting their battles on the sea, land or in the sky. In 490 BC, Persian and Greek armies slaughtered each other at Marathon. Ghostly soldiers of both armies have been seen re-enacting the battle.

Somehow their – usually – violent deaths imprint onto the areas where they died, and their ghosts are seen by some (but not by all) mortal beings. The locations where they are seen change over the years – roads and buildings are built on the original sites. For example, ghostly Roman soldiers march along their ancient roads, but are at the same level when they were alive – this explains why ghosts are seen suspended, or moving in mid air.

Not all ghosts are the result of violent deaths – some are events where men, women, children and animals die of disease, starvation, drowning, murder or natural death: victims of the Four Horsemen of the Apocalypse, War, Plague, Famine and Death – the four agents of destruction in Revelations 6.

The author (a Celtic/Viking Scottish Highlander), when he was serving in the Royal Air Force at RAF Netheravon (a First World War airfield) in the Forties, saw the dark, ghostly figure of a First World War pilot in flying clothing standing at the foot of his bed. When spoken to by the author, the figure abruptly disappeared.

This incident and several others – all personal – gave rise to an interest in the occult, which has been researched over the last sixty years. During my twenty-four years' regular and reserve service in the Royal Air Force, and my thirty-one years' police service, I collected a mass of evidence, most of which is in this book, told to me by people who were there! When I visit an old airfield or other site, I always make for the nearest pub! And there, even now, I collect tales of the paranormal – most witnesses like to tell of their experiences.

The conclusion reached was that the mass of evidence of existence after death is too much to ignore. The classic case of proof came from members of the dead crew of the crashed British airship R101 during séances. It revealed that the crash disaster was due to the R101's design and construction. The names 'Eckener' and 'SL8' featured in the séances – the author immediately recognised these as the name of a German pioneer in airship design, and the code for the Schuttee-Lanz airship the SL8. No medium could have known these. However, the Court of Enquiry ignored the highly technical design evidence of the R101 obtained during the séances, which could only have been made by aviation experts in the field of airships

When I was demobilised from the Royal Air Force, I moved to a South Coast town and bought a house. At the rear of the house, I built a garage with a heavy up-and-over door – it was impossible for the wind to lift it. During the long, hot summer of 1975, I returned from duty at a police station and drove my car into my driveway. I stopped by my front door to let my wife out, and as I did so I noticed the up-and-over door of my garage was down. I got back into my car, and drove forward some 20 feet – suddenly the up-and-over steel door swung up and locked in its up position. Without thinking, I drove forward and parked in the garage. I sat in the car and thought, 'Who lifted and opened the door?' There was no wind and no one else there. It was as though some hand from above had lifted it up. I had not been drinking! I had just finished duty at a police station where I had twenty-five constables under my command!

Oddly, that very day I had been thinking of an experience I had in Aberdeenshire before I joined the Royal Air Force. When I was seventeen years of age, I lived by the River Don in Aberdeenshire. I had a friend named Gordon Farman who lived nearby. His father had bought a small boat from Norwegians who had used it during the Second World War to cross the North Sea and escape from German-occupied Norway. Gordon and his father and brother decided to sail the boat to Newburgh, some 20 miles north of the River Don. I could have gone with them but – somehow – I did not want to. Again for some unknown reason, I watched the small boat sail away towards the North Sea until it was out of sight. I had never done this before. Later the same day, I heard from my distraught sister that the boat had capsized crossing the Newburgh Bar, and my friend Gordon and his father and brother had all drowned. Had I been on that boat, I would not have been writing this some sixty years later!

However, on 14 August 1981, while serving in Dorset Police, I was sent by a radio message to a house in Bournemouth, where I met one of my officers. The occupants of the house and many neighbours were standing outside the house in a state of shock.

I was told that there was something strange going on in the house, and I entered to investigate. In spite of the warm August sunshine, it was deathly cold inside. I saw that the television was lying on the floor, and the kitchen floor was covered in broken glass and china. As I moved further in, I saw the kitchen cabinet fall over and crash to the floor – I was the only person in the house. Drawing on my knowledge of the supernatural, I uttered an abjuration in Latin: '*Fundamenta ejus in montibus santci!*' The temperature seemed to drop several degrees more. As all was quiet, I went outside to confer with the owners. They told me that objects had been flying about the room, kitchen and hallway. A priest was contacted, and agreed to hold a service of exorcism, which ended with all present reciting the Lord's Prayer. He talked about the forces of evil that he had felt in the house, then left. Later, a spokesman for the College of Psychic Studies in London said it was a classic case of poltergeist activity.

Another odd coincidence was that when I was researching the ghost story of the First World War German U-boat U65, I consulted my extensive library and found that the only photograph I had of a German U-boat was the Second World War U33. I remembered that my uncle James Wood, a deep-sea fisherman sailing out of Fleetwood in the steam trawler *Sulby*, had been lost at sea in 1939, believed sunk by a mine. I consulted the Deutches U-Boot Museum in Cuxhaven, Germany, a friend, Jak Mallman,

Second World War U-boat U33, which sunk the steam trawler *Sulby* on 21 November 1939. The author's uncle died when U33 opened fire.

and Peter Sharpe, author of the *U-Boat Fact File*. I found that my Uncle James Wood's unarmed fishing trawler had been shelled and sunk by the deck gun of the U33 on 21 November 1939. My uncle died in the murderous attack, and went down with the *Sulby*. The U33 was depth-charged to the surface by the Royal Navy on 12 February 1940 in the Firth of Clyde. Twenty-five of the crew were killed and seventeen taken prisoner.

Alan C. Wood

Bournemouth 2010

Maritime Ghosts and Legends

The Viking Ghost Long Ship

In the Norse Viking era, when a warrior died, a longship was used as a funeral pyre. The dead warrior was placed on a bier amidships, and wood placed around him. The longship was taken out to sea, and the wooden funeral pyre set alight. South Walsham, Norfolk, is reputed to be the scene of a ghostly example: the burning, Viking longship funeral of a jarl. As it sails, it slowly sinks out of sight.

The author was born on the north coast of Scotland, and can still remember, as a very small boy, being taken one dark evening by his seafaring parents to a headland overlooking the Moray Firth. As he watched, he saw an old Scottish wooden fishing vessel hull being towed out to sea, with the flush deck piled high with wood and tar barrels. The vessel was set alight with flaming torches as it was cast adrift on the Moray Firth until the fire reached the water line, and the vessel sank out of sight.

This was a folk memory of the ancient Viking custom of burning a longboat with the dead bodies of Viking warriors aboard so that they would go to Valhalla, and their spirits could sail again for ever.

The Vikings who settled in Scotland burned their longships to indicate that they were settlers, not going to pillage and rape, and intending to remain in the local population. This is still commemorated in Shetland on the annual (last Tuesday of January) ceremony of Up Helley Aa, when a thirty-foot-long model wooden longship is burned with great ceremony.

Merlin's Prophecy

In ancient Cornwall, Merlin the magician prophesied that one day the town of Mousehole (pronounced 'Mouzel') would be attacked and burnt to the ground. In 1595, the prophecy came true when a fleet of Spanish ships attacked Mousehole and razed it to the ground with but one house – the Keigwin Arms inn – left standing. The old inn is now a private house, and on the quay is a stone named Merlin's Rock.

Warlake Hill Ghosts

Warlake Hill, near Axminster, Devon, is haunted by a host of ghosts who appear to be from the Saxon era. Local tales tell of battles fought at part of the hill known as the Kingsfield – the name derives from a battle in which five kings were slaughtered. The main legend has it that on the nights of the full moon warrior ghosts rise from out of the ground, and the rattling of chains can be heard as they are all manacled. They clank in their chains to a small stream named the lake, drink their fill, and return to their graves, then disappear back into the ground of the Kingsfield.

'Jack the Painter'

Blockhouse Point, Portsmouth – home of the British navy – is haunted by a naval sailor, 'Jack the Painter' (James Aitken), who was hanged at the yardarm for treason and arson in 1776. He had been accused of anti-royal behaviour, and of setting fire to the King's Ropehouse. Aitken was hanged from a ship's mizzenmast, then taken down and chained to a gibbet at Blockhouse Point at the entrance to Portsmouth Harbour, and left to rot for many years as a deterrent to other naval sailors. The sound of Aitken's gibbet chains are said to be heard when storm winds blow. An obelisk on Clarence Pier marks the place where a murderer sailor, John Felton, was hung in chains in 1628. The ghosts of sailors wearing a 'full set' of whiskers, which makes them of comparatively recent origin, haunt the King's Bastion.

Nancy's Sailor Lover

A farmer's daughter named Nancy fell in love with a young sailor named William - both from the village of Porthgwarra, near Land's End, Cornwall. The match was forbidden by Nancy's parents, so the lovers plighted their troth by vowing to meet again, in this world or the next, come what may. William sailed away in his ship, and was never seen again. The faithful Nancy became unbalanced, and sat on the rocks watching the sea for the return of her lover. One night, she was seen on the rocks with what appeared to be a sailor; with the tide coming in and covering the rocks, Nancy and the sailor stood up, walked into the water, and vanished. Shortly afterwards, it was found that William's ship had sunk with the loss of all on board on the day that Nancy had vanished. The mortal Nancy and the spirit of her drowned sailor lover William had been reunited – true to their pact.

Ghostly Bells Under the Sea

The sea off Forrabury, Cornwall, has a legend of church bells ringing under the sea. The legend is that new church bells were cast and sent by sea to Forrabury, but the captain of the ship carrying the bells was prone to use bad language. As his ship neared Forrabury, he began to curse and swear, whereupon a tempest blew up and the ship foundered with all hands. The legend also says that residents have seen ghostly boats being rowed out to where the ship sank with the cargo of church bells.

In Penzance, Cornwall stands The Dolphin Inn on the harbour side, built before 1588, and the maritime quarters of Sir John Hawkins as he prepared to fight the Spanish Armada. The old inn has a seafaring ghost, said to be that of a heavily-built sea captain dressed in a tricorn hat, and with lace ruffles round his neck. His heavy boots make loud treads on the old inn's wooden floors. (Courtesy of my ex-RAF friend's tales from Devon and Cornwall)

Drake: Sailor and Magician

Sir Francis Drake became a legend in the sixteenth century when he reputedly sold his soul to the Devil in exchange for the storm which contributed to the defeat of the Spanish Armada; prior to this, he wanted to marry Elizabeth Sydenham at Stogumber, Somerset, but was refused permission by Elizabeth's father. Elizabeth was paired off with a man selected by her parents, but as she was about to enter the church at Stogumber, a cannonball fell from the sky with a roar into the churchyard. The superstitious wedding guests took this as a sign of Drake's powers, firing a cannonball from his far-off ship to stop the wedding. The wedding was stopped, and Drake returned and married Elizabeth in 1585. The cannonball was in fact a small meteorite.

Drake's statue, Plymouth. (*Devon County Council, Rachel Mildon*)

The Spaniards believed that Drake had magical powers, and possessed a mirror with which he could see their ships and lie in wait for them. He was also said to be able to create ships by whittling a piece of wood, then throwing the chips into the water, where they became warships.

Drake's home was Buckland Abbey, and on buying it in 1582 he caused extensions to be added. The extensions are said to have been completed in three nights with the help of the Devil, who claimed payment by condemning Drake's ghost to drive a black hearse pulled by four headless horses – followed by headless hounds – on moonless stormy nights along the Tavistock to Plymouth road for ever. Another haunting-place of Drake's is Nutwell Court – the family home of the Drakes after his death.

Drake's drum, which now rests in Buckland Abbey – built in 1278 – is said to sound when England is in danger. In 1596, as he lay dying of fever off Puerto Bello, Panama, Drake ordered that his drum, sword and bible be returned to England and placed in Buckland Abbey, Devon, and that after death he would return to aid England in her time of need if the drum were beaten. As he was buried at sea his drum was beaten, and since then human hands have not beaten it. Devonians believe that Drake came back from the dead twice, reincarnated as Admiral Robert Blake and Admiral the Lord Nelson.

The drum is reputed to have sounded: on the eve of the battle of Trafalgar (21 October 1805); before the outbreak of the First World War; and triumphantly again on 21 November 1918, when the German Grand

Drake's Drum, Buckland Abbey, Devon. (*Plymouth City Museum*)

Surrendered German fleet, Scapa Flow, 21 November 1918. The High Seas Fleet was scuttled 21 June 1919.

Fleet surrendered to the British Fleet at Scapa Flow. As the German fleet approached the waiting British warships, a drum was heard beating on the British flagship *Royal Oak*. The Admiral in command ordered three searches of the ship, but no drum or drummer was ever found on board. The drum only stopped beating when the German Fleet had officially surrendered.

In 1939, just before the Second World War erupted, the villagers of the Devon village of Coombe Sydenham heard Drake's Drum beating. During the British retreat from Dunkirk in 1940, the drum was heard beating. In the Second World War, the drum was heard beating during the Battle of Britain in 1940, which the Royal Air Force won although out-numbered by the German Luftwaffe.

Raleigh's Ghost

The Elizabethan sailor Sir Walter Raleigh at one time owned Sherborne Castle, Dorset, and his ghost is said to walk through the castle and grounds every 28 September – St Michael's Eve. After his walk, he disappears near a tree known as Raleigh's Oak.

Raleigh also haunts the Tower of London, where he was imprisoned in 1616, and later executed by beheading at Westminster Old Palace Yard, on 29 October 1618, at the age of sixty-eight. His ghost appears near the so-called 'Raleigh's Walk', by the Bloody Tower.

Disaster on the Gilstone Reef

On 22 October 1701, Admiral Sir Cloudesly Shovell, in command of HMS *Association* and three other English warships, was sailing in bad weather unknowingly towards the notorious Gilstone Reef, off the Isles of Scilly. One of his sailors – a local man – tried to warn Shovell of the impending reef, but was hanged at the yardarm for his daring to speak out. As he swung from the yardarm, the sailor laid a curse on Shovell with his dying breath - that he and all the others would die on the Gilstone Reef.

The four warships struck the Gilstone in a raging storm, and over 2,000 sailors drowned. Shovell was washed ashore alive, but was robbed by the old woman wrecker who found him. Seeing Shovel's sapphire rings, she hacked off his fingers then buried him alive in the sand. On her deathbed, the old woman confessed to the theft of the rings. A stone monument now marks the spot where his body was found, minus his ringed fingers. His ghost is said to haunt the reef and shore looking for his missing ringed fingers. His sailor crewmembers roam the area as ghosts – especially when storms rage over the Isles of Scilly.

Captain Kidd's Ghost

Captain William Kidd – a Scotsman born in Greenock in 1645 – in spite of his reputation, was a small-scale pirate when he was hanged, protesting his innocence, at Execution Dock, Wapping, London, on 23 May 1701, for the murder of one William Moore, and piracy. Pirate he was, but he started as a respectable trader with a sloop named *Antegona*. Several businessmen talked him into becoming a pirate hunter, bought him a well-gunned frigate named *Adventure* and found a crew. Their return was to be a share of the profits taken from the pirate ships he captured.

The frigate *Adventure* was unusual in that it could be rowed if becalmed, and so he could capture other becalmed ships. Kidd sailed *Adventure* into the Indian Ocean and looked for treasure-laden pirate ships to capture. After six months he found none and turned to being a pirate himself, attacking and capturing French ships, taking considerable treasure from them. In 1698 he captured an English ship, the *Quedah*, and converted her to his own piratical use.

The following year, 1699, Kidd sailed to America, and anchored off Gardiner's Island, which is north of Long Island Bay. On a beach he and his crew buried the bulk of his pirate treasure. Kidd then sailed into Long Island Bay, New York, and was arrested when he visited Boston. America was still under British rule; he was taken to England, and put on trial for piracy, principally of the English ship *Quedah*. He was found guilty and sentenced to death by hanging in Execution Dock, Wapping, London. In America, the British Government secretly located Kidd's treasure on the beach on Gardiner's Island and shipped it to London.

When dead, Kidd's body was coated with tar to preserve it, then taken to the Thames, hoisted on a gibbet and left for the tide to wash over. This was meant to be a warning to others that hanging was the penalty for piracy. Contemporary reports allege that a dark figure was seen coming out of the Thames at Wapping and disappearing. The same dark figure, said to be the ghost of Captain Kidd, has been seen over the years at Wapping. The ship Captain Kidd used in his piracy has been seen as a ghost ship sailing off the New England coast with Kidd aboard, still searching for his treasure buried on Gardiner's island.

Another pirate, Jean Lafitte, haunts the sea off Galveston, Texas, where his pirate ship sank in 1820.

Phantom Ships, Castles, and Islands in the Sky and Sea

Irish folklore abounds with tales of phantom ships and navies in the skies and waters over and around Ireland. Tales are told of Norse longships with sails hoisted, but sailing against the wind, in Galway Bay and harbour in 1161. In the autumn of 1798 at Croagh, County Mayo, the local inhabitants saw a fleet of British warships in the sky over their heads.

On 18 July 1820, the sailing ship *Baffin*, under the command of a Captain Scoresby, was sailing off the then largely unknown west coast of Greenland on a surveying expedition. When Scoresby was examining the coast with the aid of his telescope, he saw large, ancient buildings, castles and other strange buildings on the coast. He later deposed that the buildings were real and not ghostly. There were no such buildings on the west coast of Greenland in 1820.

During the nineteenth century, several sailors swore that they had landed on ghostly islands, named the Green Meadows of Enchantment, located in the Bristol Channel somewhere between Somerset and Pembroke, and joined in a ghostly celebration. When the sailors departed, the islands disappeared. Some humans, but not all, can see the islands – strangely, people aboard aircraft have seen them from the air.

Cornwall abounds with legends of ghostly ships travelling over sea and land. Perhaps the most famous is the phantom full-rigged sailing ship of Porthcurno, Lands End, Cornwall, which in 1835 was seen to enter Porthcurno harbour against the wind and tide, then travel – a few feet above the ground – till it reached Chywidden, where it vanished into thin air.

During the eighteenth century, a ghostly schooner was sighted west of St Ives Head, Cornwall. The foreign-looking ship appeared to be in distress and was carrying a light on her bows. Her masts and rigging were coated with ice, as though she had been in Arctic weather. Local fishermen rowed out to aid or rescue the schooner and came up so close that the crew on board could be clearly seen. As the fishermen's boat came alongside, one rescuer put his hand out to grasp the schooner's lower rigging, but there was nothing there! The schooner had vanished into thin air! Cornish legends say that a sighting usually portends some maritime disaster. A ghostly lugger with sails set has been seen in Croft Pascoe Poole, on the Goonhilly Downs. At St Levan, another ghost ship appears, and sails from the sea overland before disappearing inland.

Oulton Broad, Norfolk, is haunted by the ghost of a large barge-type wherry boat named *Mayfly*, the crew of which died in mysterious circumstances, leaving only the cabin boy as a survivor.

The Ghost of Captain Madero

Captain Porfino Madero was the first captain of the Mexican ship *Chalchibuitlicue*, which had a regular sea run from Mazatlan, Mexico, to San Diego, California, United States and return. After a long career at sea, Captain Madero died in 1841.

Late in 1852, the *Chalchibuitlicue*, commanded by a former Lieutenant in the United States Navy, was en route from Mazatlan to San Diego, when a vicious winter storm blew up off San Quintin, Mexico. The *Chalchbuitlicue* was yawing, pitching, rolling and rising in the violent seas that caused her to lose her rudder, which rendered her steering useless. To add to the crew's troubles, most of her rigging fell on the midships deck, killing two crew, and a sail spar fell on the captain's head, rendering him unconscious.

Driven by the storm, the ship surged out of control towards the foaming rocks and a certain death for all aboard. Suddenly, from a below-decks companionway, a man dressed in a Mexican Navy uniform became visible amid the spume and spray of the sea. The uniformed officer assumed command from the bridge, and ordered the crew to bring the ship into wind by making a jury-rig rudder. The *Chalchbuitlicue* came under control, and sailed into the safety of San Diego Roads. When the captain came to, the Mexican naval officer had disappeared.

The *Chalchbuitlicue* captain had no idea who the man in Mexican naval uniform was. He did not appear on his ship's crew roll or passenger manifest. The captain recorded all the details in his Ship's Log. However, some of the crew of the *Chalbuitlicue* who had sailed with its first master, Captain Madero, identified him as the phantom officer in the Mexican naval uniform who had saved them from a watery grave.

Some years later, the National University of Mexico found the ship's log, with the entry about the unknown officer in Mexican naval uniform, in Mexican Shipping Archives – an official proof that the ghost of Captain Madero had come to the rescue of the stricken vessel. (Courtesy of US Naval Institute Press)

A Sailor Sentry Ghost

During the Napoleonic Wars, French prisoners of war were held in various locations in the south of England, from Dartmoor to Chatham. The old St Mary's Barracks, Chatham, has the ghost of a sailor gaoler who, legend has it, was murdered by escaping French prisoners of war. The ghostly gaoler has a crippled leg, and uses a primitive wooden crutch for support as he makes his rounds of Cumberland Block in the barracks. Cell room No. 34 is his usual haunt, as he was beaten to death near this room, but he also haunts the ramparts during the Middle Watch (midnight to 4.00 a.m.). The staff of the old barracks saw him in 1947 and 1949. The dockyard at Chatham has a naval ghost: none other than Admiral the Lord Horatio Nelson as a young man, prior to his achieving greatness. His ship HMS *Victory* was built at the Chatham yard, and Nelson, as a young man, joined his first ship there in 1770. His ghost is said to walk through the old dockyard, and is of a young man in naval uniform, uninjured by the battle actions that deprived him of his right arm and eye.

The Three Sailors' Ghosts

At Porlock Weir, Somerset, the bodies of three sailors were washed ashore. One sailor was black, one was a young cabin boy and the other middle-aged. The local authorities made enquiries without result, and the three were buried in Marsh Field, near the beach where they had been found. Three ghosts, thought to be those of the sailors, have been repeatedly seen in the area by local inhabitants.

Porlock Weir, Somerset. (*Iris Hardwick, courtesy of Somerset County Council*)

A Canadian Ghostly Man o' War

Off Cap d'Espoir, in the Gulf of St Lawrence, Canada, a ghostly fully-rigged man o' war, reputed to be an English flagship sent from England in 1710 to neutralise by gunfire the French forts on the Cap, but which was wrecked on the rocks beneath the forts, sails onto the rocks again and again.

The flagship carries scores of armed, red-clothed soldiers and blue-clad sailors. All her lights are showing. At the bows stand a naval officer and a woman, frantically pointing towards the rocky shore towards which the man o' war is heading. Screams are heard from the doomed vessel, and all her lights go out, then she vanishes.

The Ghostly Naval Officer in York Minster

Early in the nineteenth century, several parties of visitors were visiting York Minster; among them was a small party of two sisters and their father, who were detached and away from the main parties. The evening light in the Minster was poor, but enough to see by. Suddenly, the two sisters and their father saw a man dressed in a British naval officer's uniform approaching their front. He seemed to appear from nowhere. As the naval officer drew closer, his face became visible in the gloom. One of the sisters became distressed and her father turned to assist her, as did the other sister.

York Minster. (*Dayfield Graphics, York*)

The naval officer was now but a few feet away from the sister in distress, who had became acutely distressed and was breathing heavily. The naval officer approached the woman in distress, and whispered in her ear 'There is another place'. He then turned and walked away out of sight.

The father told his other daughter to look after her distressed sister, and searched for the naval officer. Nothing was found; there was no sign or sound of him. The father asked his distressed daughter what was the matter of her distress. Painfully, she replied that his son, her brother, and a sailor was dead, drowned at sea. The father asked how she knew this, and she said that her brother and she had made a pact: that the first to die would appear to the survivor – no matter how far they were apart in the world. The man in naval uniform was his son and her brother.

A few weeks later, the sad news was received that the son had indeed drowned at sea. The time of his death was at exactly the time he had been seen in York Minster by his father and two sisters.

The American Officers' Deadly Duel

Decatur House, Layfayette Square, Washington DC, USA, is now a museum, but in 1820 was the home of Commodore Stephen Decatur, United States Navy. Decatur was an American naval hero, famed for his actions at sea, but he and a Commodore James Barron, also of the Navy, became enemies. Barron was arraigned before a court martial for an unlawful action at sea against the Royal Navy which led to the War of 1812. Decatur was a member of the court martial, which convicted Barron and sentenced him to be suspended from the Navy for five years. Baron brooded on his suspension, and even though he was reinstated to the Navy on half pay, he nursed a hatred of Decatur. After Barron made several personal slanderous attacks on Decatur, a duel of honour was arranged for the morning of 14 March 1820, in a field at Bladensburg, Maryland.

At dawn on the appointed duel day, Decatur, with his flintlock single-shot pistol in a black case, went with his second, Captain William Bainbridge, to the field. Each officer took ten paces then levelled their flintlock pistols at each other. On the count of two, both fired. Barron fell to the ground, wounded in the hip. Decatur fell, mortally wounded in his right chest, and died. He was given a naval funeral with all naval honours.

A year later, his ghost was seen at dawn, looking out from the bedroom window of Decatur House, and he was seen leaving the house carrying a black pistol case under his left arm – re-enacting his last journey to the duelling field.

Ghostly Press Gangs

Colyton Crescent, Exeter, Devon, has some fine Georgian houses and which, around the late 1700s and early 1800s, belonged to a Royal Navy Admiral. While the Admiral was away at sea fighting the French fleets, the local area around the Crescent was a favourite haunt of local Press Gangs, who snatched men off the streets and pressed them into Royal Navy service against their will. The local men snatched were supposed to be fit and able citizens, but the Press Gangs, who were paid by results, seized any man they could find on the streets. The local Devonians were stoutly against this practice, and resisted the Press Gangs by fighting back. Legend has it that several members of Press Gangs were killed, their bodies thrown into the nearby River Exe. Their ghosts are heard fighting and screaming, and have been seen inside several nearby Georgian houses which are reputed to be haunted.

Colyton Crescent and the River Exe. (*Devon County Council, Rachel Mildon*)

The Royal Marine Ghost

On 24 March 1878, the Royal Navy twenty-six-gun frigate *Eurydice*, built in 1843, foundered in a sudden squall and northerly snowstorm off the Isle of Wight coast, opposite Lucombe Chine. She was carrying some 300 crew, which included a complement of Royal Marines, among whom was a twenty-four-year-old Royal Marine, James Turner, who had a young sister in Darlington. Of the 300 crew, only two survived; the remainder, including James Turner, drowned as the ship went down.

That night, James Turner's young sister saw the ghostly figure of a Marine standing by her bedroom door, dripping wet; she recognised him as her brother, but, at this time, did not know he had drowned when he went down with his ship. As she watched in horror, the ghostly figure gradually disappeared.

The ghostly form of HMS *Eurydice* still haunts the waters off the Isle of Wight as a fully-rigged sailing warship. In the early 1930s, a submarine almost collided with a ghostly fully-rigged sailing warship off the Isle of Wight – was it HMS *Eurydice*?

The Haunted HMS *Asp*

HMS *Asp* started her sea life as an old-fashioned twin-paddle ship named *Fury*, and was used as a mail packet ship by the Royal Mail until 1837. The Royal Navy bought *Fury,* redesigned her as a survey ship, and renamed her HMS *Asp*. Seamen regard it as bad luck to rename a ship, and this came true when reports began to circulate that she was haunted.

In 1850, a Captain Alldridge, Royal Navy, took command of HMS *Asp*, and as he took over, the Superintendent of Shipyards, Pembroke Dock, Wales told him that none of his workmen would work on the ship, as it was reputed to be haunted. Captain Alldridge decried the stories of *Asp* being haunted as nonsense, and said that he did not believe in such tales. HMS *Asp* was fitted out, and took up station on the River Dee, Chester, to commence her survey of the sea area, with Captain Alldridge in command.

After duty, Captain Alldridge would retire to his sea cabin to relax and read. He began to hear noises from the aft cabin, which was opposite his cabin. He investigated and examined the aft cabin, but there was no one therein. Alldridge went back to his cabin, and the noises started up again, as though some drunken sailor was staggering about and shouting. He roared out, 'Don't make such a noise out there', and immediately the noises stopped. As he settled down to read the noises started up again, but louder; thinking it was his Steward, he called out 'Don't make such a noise Steward', and the noises stooped at once. A few minutes later, they started again and the Captain rushed out of his cabin into the aft cabin. It was empty.

For some nights, when the Captain retired for the night and had fallen asleep, he was awakened by the sounds of drawers being opened and closed in the empty aft cabin. Again he checked the aft cabin, and again it was empty.

When HMS *Asp* was at anchor and the two-man night-duty watch had been set, the captain retired to his cabin, but was awakened by the Quartermaster who called him on deck. Quaking, the sailor said that the lookout had seen the ghostly figure of a woman standing on the starboard paddle-box, pointing with one finger upwards. The Captain looked, but there was no figure of a woman on the paddle-box. After this incident, the ghostly figure of a young woman was frequently seen, and always accompanied by the smell of perfume. Such was the atmosphere of fear on board that the crew began to apply for transfer or discharge from the Royal Navy. These were granted, but the Captain stood his ground and stayed with HMS *Asp*. The ghost began to get bolder, and one night when the Captain was asleep, he felt a ghostly, cold, clammy hand touching his leg over the bedclothes.

In 1857, when the ship was at Pembroke Dock, a shore sentry saw the ghostly figure of a white-clad woman standing on the starboard paddle-box with her arm pointing upwards. As the sentry looked, the ghostly figure left the paddle-box and started to glide towards him. He challenged the apparition with the usual challenge, 'Halt, who goes there?' Ignoring the sentry and his challenge, the ghostly figure came at him and passed through his body. In sheer panic and terror, the sentry ran to the Guardhouse, and as he did so another sentry, who had seen the incident, fired his gun to rouse the Guard. As the sentries watched in terror, the ghostly figure made its way to a nearby churchyard and vanished – still with her finger pointing upwards.

From then on, all sentries were ordered to patrol in twos and report all sighting of the ghost, but she never reappeared.

Enquiries were made into the history of HMS *Asp* before she became a Royal Navy ship, and it was found that when she was the mail packet *Fury*, a young woman had been brutally murdered in the aft cabin by having her throat cut and slashed. Her murder was never solved. Finally, HMS *Asp* was sent to the wreckers' yard in 1881.

The Ghostly Workman of the *Great Eastern*

The *Great Eastern* steam/sail ship was the brainchild of Isambard Kingdom Brunel (born 1806, died 1859). She was 692 feet long, displaced 22,500 tons, carried some 6,500 square yards of sail, and had a 24-foot propeller, plus two 58-foot-diameter paddle wheels. The huge ship was the largest ever built, and was designed by Brunel for the England to Australia run. Because of her great size, she was to be built and launched sideways on the river Thames.

Some 2,000 workmen of all trades were employed on building the steel double hull, and – perhaps inevitably – fatal accidents began to happen. Five workmen died working on the hull, and one riveter went missing when working on the midships section of the hull. His fellow workers reported him missing but, though a search was made, no trace of him was found.

On 3 November 1857, the *Great Eastern* was ready for launching, but she stuck on the Thames mud, and it was not until 9 September 1859 that she was afloat and ready for her intended role. As she lay afloat, some of the crew complained that there was persistent hammering from inside the hull. The hammering appeared to come from the inner shell of the double hull of the ship. No cause for the hammering was found. Some of her crew began to say that she was haunted, and that would account for her run of

SS *Great Eastern*.

bad luck. Finally, the *Great Eastern* got under way and sailed towards the open sea, but after a few hours one of her smokestacks was riven apart by an explosion in the engine room which killed six engineers. The sounds of hammering were heard over the years, and became the ghost of the *Great Eastern*.

The *Great Eastern* made several crossings to America, but for some reason she was not a business success. Eventually, the monster ship was sold for scrap in 1887. As she was towed to Henry Bath & Sons breaker's yard at Birkenhead, the sound of hammering from within the hull was heard yet again.

During January 1889, the *Great Eastern* began to be reduced to scrap metal. Starting topside, the great ship was ripped apart by the wrecking crew. Reaching the inner shell of the double hull, it was said that the wrecking crew broke into a sealed section on the port side. To their horror, they saw a skeleton lying on its side, clutching a carpetbag filled with rusty riveter's tools. It was the skeleton of the missing riveter who had somehow become trapped between the double hull thirty years before. His frantic efforts to attract attention to release him from his metal tomb had been to no avail. He died a horrible death, after which his ghost had continued his hammering – perhaps to affect its own release. It has never been confirmed that this was the case, but in any event hammering was heard from somewhere inside the ship by hundreds of passengers and crew. Perhaps it was another ghost somehow associated with the *Great Eastern* during its lifetime.

The Ghost in Berkeley Square

In December 1887, HMS *Penelope*, a frigate, docked at her home port of Portsmouth on Christmas Eve, and her crew was given shore leave. Two Able Seamen, Edward Blunden and Robert Martin, made for the bright lights of London to enjoy its pleasures with the little money they had in their possession. They could not find any cheap lodgings, so looked for somewhere to sleep for the night. Aimlessly walking the darkened streets of Piccadilly, they found themselves in Berkeley Square, where they spotted a To Let sign outside No. 50, which looked derelict and unoccupied. Gaining entry, they made a cursory search and found a bedroom on the second floor, where they decided to bed down. Both dropped into a restless sleep, but were awakened by the sound of heavy footsteps outside the closed bedroom door. Now both were wide awake, and saw the bedroom door slowly open and a huge, dark figure come towards them. It had no definite outline and made no sound. Panic-stricken, the two sailors tried to escape, but the apparition seized Blunden. Martin, terror-stricken, ran out of the bedroom, leaving Blunden struggling with the shapeless figure. Martin went down the stairs at speed and ran into a patrolling police constable. Blurting out what had happened, Martin and the constable went into No. 50. The dead body of Blunden lay at the bottom of the stairs – his neck was broken, and his face contorted in terror.

The two sailors had entered one of London's most haunted houses. It had been haunted for many years, and had a fearsome reputation of being haunted by some shapeless, slithering mass of a being. A Sir Robert Warboys, a member of White's Gentlemen's Club, accepted a wager that he would not spend a night in the haunted house. Sir Robert took with him several of his friends and the owner of the house, but they had to stay on the ground floor and Sir Robert had to occupy the second floor bedroom, which had a bell-pull to call servants. He also took a loaded revolver. Sir Robert went to bed about 11.15 p.m.; that was the last time his friends saw him alive. Forty minutes later, his friends heard the sound of the servant bell jangling, then a gun being fired. His friends ran upstairs to the bedroom, where they found Sir Robert lying in bed with the revolver in his hand. One shot had been fired. He had died in terror, but not from a bullet – he had a contorted face, protruding eyes and teeth clenched like a dog snarling.

Another report is that, when the house was occupied, the daughter of the occupants was engaged to a young Army officer. The officer scoffed at the report of a ghost, and volunteered to spend the night in the bedroom supposed to be haunted. He instructed the family that he would ring the servant bell twice if he was in need of assistance. Nervously, the family occupants waited downstairs. Just before midnight, the officer entered the haunted bedroom, taking his army revolver with him. On the stroke of midnight the servant's bell rang once, then two minutes later rang again, violently this time. Rushing upstairs, the family heard the sound of a gunshot, and on entering the haunted bedroom found the army officer dead from a bullet from his army revolver. There was no one else in the room. The army officer had shot himself in terror of what he had seen.

Admirals' Ghosts

The National Maritime Museum at Greenwich is haunted by a ghost or ghosts, one of which is believed to be that of Admiral John Byng, who was court-martialled at Portsmouth, allegedly for negligence in commanding his fleet in battle with the French. The sentence of the court martial was death by firing squad on the quarterdeck of HMS *Monarch*, such sentence being duly carried out on 14 March 1747. The tall, frock-coated, black-clad ghostly figure of Byng has been seen ascending the Tulip staircase, then vanishing when he reaches the top. Before becoming the National Maritime Museum, the seventeenth-century building was known as the Queen's House. In 1966, a visitor took a photograph of the Tulip staircase, and when the film was developed, it showed what appeared to be a ghostly figure on the staircase.

On 22 June 1893, Vice Admiral Sir George Tryon was on the bridge of his flagship HMS *Victoria*, and in command of the Mediterranean Fleet of eight battleships and five cruisers engaged in fleet evolutions off the coast of Syria. HMS *Camperdown* divided Tryon's fleet into two columns, one led by his flagship. The exercise planned was for the two columns to steam ahead at nine knots on a parallel course – a mere six cables length apart – then turn inwards, and steam on the reverse course. HMS *Camperdown* commenced her turn inwards, but Tryon, who seemed to be in some form of a trance, did not give the order for HMS *Victoria* to turn until it was too late to avoid a collision. *Camperdown*'s bows tore into *Victoria*'s starboard side, causing her to founder with the loss of 358 sailors, including Tryon, who went down with his ship.

The same day, 2,000 miles away, Lady Tryon was giving a tea-party at her London home when the figure of Vice Admiral Sir George Tryon, in full uniform, walked down the ornate staircase, in full view of his horror-stricken wife and their assembled guests, strode across the crowded room, opened a closed door then vanished. Lady Tryon knew it was impossible for her husband to be in London, and knew her husband was in the Mediterranean on his flagship.

The Flying Dutchman

The ghostly, fully-rigged brig known as the Flying Dutchman appears off the coasts of South Africa, particularly the Cape of Good Hope, but she has also been sighted off Australia. The legend began in the seventeenth century when a Dutch captain, Hendrik van Decken, sailed in a fully-rigged brig from Amsterdam, bound for the East Indies. As his ship rounded the Cape of Good Hope, a storm blew up, which normally meant reducing sail and riding out the heavy seas till the storm abated. Van Decken refused to take in sail, and carried on into the storm under full sail. It was said he was in league with the Devil and flouted the storm, which was an Act of God. God then punished van Decken and his crew by making them sail the seas forever in their ghostly ship.

King George V, when a midshipman aboard HMS *Inconstant*, saw the ghostly brig at 4.00 a.m. on 11 July 1881, off the coast of Australia, and it was entered in the ship's log. 'During the Middle Watch the so called Flying Dutchman crossed our bows. She first appeared as strange red light – as if a ship all aglow. In the midst of which light her masts, spars and sails, seemingly those of a normal brig, some 200 yards from us, stood out in strong relief as she came up close on the port bow, where also the officer of the watch from the bridge clearly saw her, as did our quarterdeck midshipman, who was sent forward at once to the forecastle to report back. But, on reaching the fo'castle, there was no vestige nor any sign of any material ship was to be seen either near or away to the horizon. The early morning as the night had been, was clear, the sea strangely calm. Thirteen persons altogether saw her. Two other ships – *Tourmaline* and *Cleopatra* – sailing on our starboard bow, flashed to ask if we had seen the strange sight'. Twelve other sailors were witnesses to the occurrence.

The appearance of the Flying Dutchman is said to portend death, and HMS *Inconstant*'s mast-head lookout, who first saw the apparition, fell to his death from the foremast cross-trees mast at 10.45 a.m. He was buried at sea at 4.15 p.m. the same day.

During the Second World War, the Flying Dutchman was sighted several times. Kriegsmarine Admiral Karl Doenitz, Hitler's Commander of U-Boats (submarines), reported officially that some of his U-boat crews had seen the ghostly Flying Dutchman whilst on war patrol. 'Certain of my U-boat crews claimed that they had seen the Flying Dutchman during their tours of duty east of Suez. When they returned to their home bases the crews said they would prefer to face the combined might of Allied warships in the North Atlantic, than know the terror a second time of being confronted by a phantom ship'.

The Ghost Galley of Clan Campbell

When the Chief of Clan Campbell (the Duke of Argyll, whose seat is at Inveraray, Scotland, by Loch Fyne) dies, an ancient, ghostly, three-man, crewed, oared galley appears on Loch Fyne, with sails furled and all flags flying. The galley is rowed over the loch, then across the ground to the Church of St Columba. On the coat of arms of the Dukedom of Argyll, which family dates back before 1294, a similar galley is depicted on the first and third quarters of the shield. The Dukes are Hereditary Admirals of the Western Coasts and Isles of Scotland. The local populace last saw the ghostly galley in 1913, when Lord Archibald Campbell died. A Campbell-tartan-clad ghostly piper and harpist can be heard when a member of the family is about to die. A ghostly army column of Cumberland's red-coated soldiers is often seen, marching six abreast along the road from Inveraray castle to Dalmally.

A First World War Ghostly U-Boat

One of twenty-four new German U-boats (submarines), the U65 was built at the Germaniawerft, Kiel, and launched on 21 March 1916, and immediately gained an evil reputation when a steel girder fell on a workman on board, killing him. Another workman died of his injuries en route to hospital. Just before the U-boat's completion, the engine room compartment filled with chloride gas fumes and three more workmen engineers died.

On her shake-down trials in the North Sea, a crewmember was lost overboard; he left the conning tower and walked, without looking left or right, straight into the cold North Sea near the island of Nordbeveland, off the Schelde. His body was never found.

The U65's captain dived the boat and she settled on the seabed, but when he gave the order to surface, the U65 would not obey her controls. For twelve hours she lay on the seabed while the crew struggled to float her upwards. As she lay immobile, deadly chloride fumes from the electric batteries began to fill the hull and slowly gas the crew. At the last minute before death – somehow – the U-boat began to rise to the surface and into the blessed fresh air.

The U65's run of death continued – her Executive Officer and five sailors were killed in a mysterious explosion when loading torpedoes, and were buried with full naval honours at Wilhelmshaven. Twelve men had so far died during the short career of the boat.

The U65 or a sister boat. (*Newnes Ltd*)

Two years later, the U65 was on patrol in the English Channel when a lookout crewmember saw a figure on the open, wave-lashed deck. The figure turned, and the lookout saw that it was the Executive Officer who had died in the torpedo explosion and was buried in the cemetery at Wilhelmshaven. Two of the crew – one called Pedersen – swore that they had seen him come aboard, walk to the bows and stand with his arms folded, staring at them. Two days later, Pedersen deserted the U-boat.

The ghostly Executive Officer's figure was seen another four times, and the reports caused an Admiral to seek help from a Pastor of the Luthern Church to exorcise the ghost. The exorcism was duly carried out at Bruge, Belgium.

In May 1918, U65 was patrolling in the Bay of Biscay, off Finisterre, when her senior gunner, named Eberhardt, saw the ghost of the Executive Officer. Eberhardt was put under close arrest, but broke out from his cell and committed suicide.

On dawn patrol the next day, a crewmember, Petty Officer Meyer, dived into the cold water and swam away, never to be seen again. The submerged U65 was depth-charged by the Royal Navy and forced to the seabed. Then the interior of the submarine began to glow with a greenish light throughout the hull. The U65 managed to surface and reach its home base, and was re-commissioned with a new commander and crew. After a refit she put to sea again.

First World War German U-Boat of the same type as U65 firing its deck gun.
(*Newnes Ltd and Elsevier Publishing*)

U65 was next seen again on the surface, by an American submarine patrolling at periscope depth on 10 July 1918 off the coast of Ireland, near Cape Clear. Closing to the attack, the American commander, looking through his periscope, saw the marking 'U65' on the conning tower side. There was no lookout crew on the U-boat, which appeared abandoned.

As the Commander watched and prepared to launch a spread salvo of his torpedoes, he saw a dark figure standing, with arms folded, on the bows of the U65. Before the American submarine could launch its torpedoes, the U65 exploded and quickly sank. As she sank, the dark figure on the bows disappeared from sight before she went to her watery grave with her crew of thirty-four men.

Addendum. The Deutches U-Boat Museum, Cuxhaven, Germany, informed me that the U65 was scuttled near Pola on 29 October 1918 ... There appears to be some confusion as to the U65 and the UB65 submarines, and there was also a UC65!

The Goodwin Sands Ghosts

Many sailors have drowned in shipwrecks on the treacherous Goodwin Sands, 5 miles east of Deal, Kent, and many alleged sightings have been reported of phantom civilian ships. The Sands are about 4 miles across and 11 miles long, and are covered to an average depth of 12 feet at high tide. It is said by locals that as many as 50,000 souls have perished on the dreaded Sands.

In 1703, the sixty-gunned warship *Shrewsbury* was lost on the Goodwins, and is reputed to reappear on the anniversary of its sinking. On the wild stormy night of 25/26 November 1703, the Goodwins swallowed four navy frigates, *Stirling Castle*, *Northumberland*, *Restoration*, and *Mary*. 1,271 sailors perished in the cold waters.

Two survivors from the *Mary* were rescued, and stated that before they went onto the deadly Sands, they had seen a ghostly sixteenth-century warship with all guns firing, and afire from stem to stern, ram their ship, pass bodily through it with any feeling of impact, then disappear into the Sands. The ghostly form of a frigate in distress was seen, two days later, by ships anchored well off the Goodwins to ride out the storm; her nameplate read *Northumberland*, and she was out of control and heading straight onto the Sands, where she disappeared once again. The *Northumberland* was seen again, some fifty years later in 1753, running without masts or sails against the wind. A Spanish galleon, *c.* 1588, is said to founder on the sands to the sound of her broadside guns firing.

A German U-boat is reputed to appear on the Sands, and legend has it that a Second World War U-boat was found on the Sands in 1939 with all the crew aboard, dead at their posts.

The Smelly Sailor Ghost

North of Faversham, Kent, is the thirteenth-century Shipwright's Arms pub, on the banks of the muddy, tidal River Swale, overlooking the marshlands of Hollow Shore. The isolated pub is reported to be the haunt of a bearded, bulging, red-eyed ghost, smelling of pungent pipe tobacco, rum and tar, and dressed in a sailor's reefer jacket with brass buttons and a black sailor's cap on his thickset head. Sometimes he is wearing a long black coat, and frequents both the pub and the shipyard nearby.

Legend has it that he is the captain of a nineteenth-century ship that sank nearby. He managed to crawl through the mud flats and hammer on the door of the house which is now the Shipwright's Arms. The occupants of the house would not open the door, and the Captain died on their doorstep during the night.

Occupants of the pub have found the Captain in their rooms during the night, and in the only bar in the pub, where the temperature drops when he appears. Other seamen's ghosts have been seen in the bar and around the boatyard nearby. According to locals, the seafaring ghosts are always walking along Hollow Shore!

The ghost of a sailor, who was murdered there in 1800, haunts the Chequers Inn at Smarden, Kent.

The Scrambling Net Ghost

The author's brother – Chief Petty Officer William George Wood, Royal Navy – was serving aboard a cruiser in the Pacific on 4 May 1941. He was off watch and asleep when a radio operator woke him and handed him a radio message from the Admiralty, London. The message read: 'Regret to inform you that your father George Wood, Merchant Navy, died today in Fleetwood Hospital, Lancashire, of wounds received at sea' CPO Wood signed for the radio message, and gathered his thoughts. Just before he had been woken, he had been dreaming that he was on the side of his ship, throwing a scrambling net over the side to our father, who was in the sea. Our father caught the net and climbed aboard at the time he died in Fleetwood Hospital.

The Sailor Ghost from HMS Royal Oak

On Sunday 3 September 1939, Great Britain declared war on Hitler's Germany, and the Second World War began. The German Navy (Kriegsmarine) placed great reliance on its submarine branch, the U-boats, as Great Britain was an island nation, and could be defeated by cutting off its war supplies by sinking its Merchant Navy with U-boats.

One such submarine was the U47 commanded by Captain Gunther Prien, who set sail from Kiel, Germany on 8 October 1939 and made for the Royal Navy's naval base at Scapa Flow in the Orkney Islands, off the north coast of Scotland.

Scapa Flow was thought to be a safe anchorage and haven for the 29,000-ton British battleship HMS *Royal Oak* which lay anchored there. All the crew were on board, including the Captain and Admiral Blagrove.

The U47 managed to enter Scapa Flow undetected during the night of 13 October 1939, and at 1.30 the next morning torpedoed the massive HMS *Royal Oak*, causing it to sink with the loss of 833 British sailors. The U47's Captain Prien navigated the submarine out of Scapa Flow undetected, and made for Kiel Naval Base, arriving there on 17 October 1939.

Dennis Bardens, the famous ghost book author, writes in his *Ghosts and Hauntings* that a lady told him that her fiancée had been serving on HMS *Royal Oak* at the time it was sunk, and during the night she had had a

HMS *Royal Oak*.

vision of him standing near her; after a minute, the vision faded away. She later found that her fiancée had been one of the 833 dead.

For sinking HMS *Royal Oak*, Hitler feted Captain Gunther Prien and his crew on 18 October 1939 in Berlin, and Prien was decorated with Hitler's award of the Knight's Cross of the Iron Cross.

On the night of the 7/8 March 1941, Captain Prien in U47 attempted to torpedo ships of a Royal Navy-escorted British convoy off Rockall. The U47 was detected and rammed by one of the escorts, HMS *Wolverine*; Captain Prien, and all forty-five members of his crew died.

A Ghostly Second World War Landing Craft

During the Second World War, the coasts of Devon were used by Allied Forces landing craft, training for the D-Day (6 June 1944) invasion of Normandy. Due to accidents, weather, and enemy action, many landing craft crew were lost. In October 1959, during a storm, a 500-ton Second World War landing craft flying the Free French flag (the double-barred Cross of Lorraine) was seen wallowing in distress off the Devon coast.

Two British warships, together with three other ships, the *Turmoil*, *Acute* and *Torquay*, were sent to assist and rescue the apparently stricken landing craft. As the rescue boats came up on the landing craft, pitching and rolling in the rough seas, the navy crews saw the landing craft was deserted, and did not answer radio or light signals. As the rescuers came about to board the deserted landing craft, it vanished into thin air.

A Ghostly Nuclear Submarine

The American Navy nuclear attack submarine USS *Thresher* (SSN–593) displaced some 4,300 tons when launched on 9 July 1960, and was the prototype of the Thresher Class of American submarines. Her nuclear reactor gave steam power to a 15,000 hp steam turbine. She could sail for some 60,000 miles without refuelling at a submerged speed of thirty-five knots, or twenty surface knots.

On 10 April 1963, *Thresher* left port for diving tests with a complement of 129 navy and civilian personnel. The next day at 9.12 a.m., *Thresher* dived to her test depth, some 230 miles east of Cape Cod where the sea depth is 1,400 fathoms.

Thresher reported by submarine phone to her surface mother ship *Skylark* that 'All was going very well'. Two minutes later, *Skylark* received another telephone message that *Thresher* was attempting to blow the ballast tanks, and that the boat was in the position up-angle. This would mean she was attempting to surface by forcing air into the water-filled ballast tanks. Five minutes later another telephone message was received by *Skylark*, but was garbled and unreadable. There were no further messages.

US Navy submarine No. 593 under way. (*US Navy and US Embassy, London*)

It is not known what depth *Thresher* had reached, but the water pressure at 6,000 feet is well over 3,700 lb per square inch. If she were at this depth, notwithstanding her pressure hull, she would have been crushed like an eggshell.

Thresher was officially declared lost with all hands in April 1963. A search group was formed to locate the submarine, and the shattered remains of *Thresher* were located on the sea floor, some 8,400 feet below the surface. (Report from United States Navy)

In the summer of 1967, a resident of Boston, Massachusetts, with his family, was sailing their yacht 220 miles from Cape Cod, off the New England coast. A large sea was running and throwing sea spray up from their yacht's bows into their faces. The experienced skipper of the yacht piloted his craft in the rough conditions with care, keeping her a few points off the strong wind, when he saw, at a cable's length off his starboard bow, a submarine surface.

Looking into the wind and spray, the five-strong family saw the name *Thresher* painted on the forward side of the submarine. The yacht skipper identified it as a United States naval submarine, and saw it was badly damaged along the waterline (*Thresher* did not have her name painted on the bow section – only her number).

As the yacht skipper and his family watched the amazing sight, they became aware that two United States Navy uniformed sailors were observing them from the apparently stricken submarine. One was on the conning tower with a telescope, and another on the bows.

Suddenly, the submarine rose bodily into the air, broke in two, and sank quickly beneath the rough running sea. The two sailors visible on the submarine did not move as the submarine sank, and went down in their positions with their boat.

The yacht skipper carried out research, and found that there had been a United States navy submarine – the USS *Thresher* – which had sunk with all hands in 1963, in the location where she had been seen sinking by him and his family. However, the USS *Thresher* did not have its name painted on the boat; it had serial number 593 on the sail (conning tower) and bows.

USS *Thresher*, submarine No. 593, perhaps as seen by witnesses as a ghostly submarine. (*US Navy and US Embassy, London*)

The American Navy Aircraft Carrier Ghost

The massive aircraft carrier the USS *James V. Forrestal* – Ship Code Serial Number 59 – saw combat duty in the American war against North Vietnamese forces. Her carrier-borne aircraft supported US ground forces against the Communist Viet Cong from 1967 until 1973.

During 1967, the *Forrestal* was cruising on operations off the coast of Vietnam when a fireball erupted on her flight deck, which was crowded with some fifty aircraft and air and ship crews. When the fire was brought under control, it was found that 134 air and ship crews had perished in the flames. Of necessity, the bodies had to be stored in the ship's refrigerators until port was reached.

Forrestal began to have tales of strange happenings; no one would venture into the ship's refrigerators where the bodies had been stored. One sailor did go into the store to get some ice cream cartons, but ran off when he felt a hand on his shoulder. There was no one else in the store! Another sailor saw a ghostly, badly-burned arm and hand appear out of a solid steel bulkhead, then disappear back into the bulkhead. No ghostly sailor was ever seen, but the incidents continued to happen, and the crew christened the supposed ghost of one of the dead crew George. The USS *Forrestal* was taken out of commission in 1993.

The Ghostly Schooner that Disappeared

The United States Coastguard's cutters patrol the Caribbean Islands to intercept drug smugglers. On a very dark, windless night off Montego Bay a USCG cutter was hove to waiting for business! As the sailors kept watch, they saw a schooner under way, with her sails billowing – but there was no wind!

The cutter put on speed and went after the schooner, which was caught in the cutter's powerful searchlights. The schooner crew could be seen putting on more sail to make their way out of the Bay.

The Coastguard cutter came alongside the schooner, and prepared to board her at arms. Before the boarding party could board the schooner, it vanished! The cutter crew could not believe their eyes, and searched the darkness. There was no schooner – it had disappeared into thin air.

The Sailor Ghost of Sandwood Bay, North-West Scottish Highlands

Sandwood Bay is 5 miles south of Cape Wrath (Wrath is the Norse Viking word for turning point for home), on the remote north-west Atlantic coast of Highland Scotland. There are no roads to the beautiful pink sands, with the nearest hamlet, Sheigra, 3 miles away. The sands are overlooked by three mountains – the nearest of which is Beinn Dearg Mhor (Big Red Mountain).

There have been numerous daylight sightings of a ghostly sailor walking the pink sands of Sandwood Bay. He is of large stature, grey-bearded, wearing a navy-blue reefer jacket with shining brass buttons, sailor's peaked cap, and black sea boots. He is reported as being of solid, lifelike appearance. The ghostly sailor strides across the desolate pink sands then disappears – he does not leave any footprints in the soft sand! One on occasion, he shouted to a local crofter (farmer) that all the driftwood on the beach was his! Therefore, he is not a silent ghost! The crofter decided that discretion was the better part of valour, and ran for his life off the haunted beach.

He was seen frequently in 1949 and 1953 at the seldom-used Sandwood Cottage near the Cape Wrath lighthouse, where fishermen and fishing

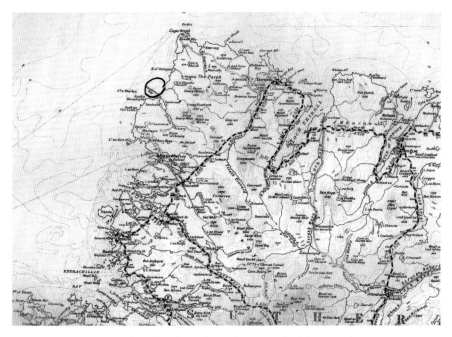

Map of north-west Scotland with Sandwood Bay marked by a circle. (*Roger Pountain and Harper Collins*)

Sandwood Bay. (*Roger E. Pountain Collection*)

parties occasionally spend the night. One night, a local fisherman decided to spend the night in the cottage. As he slept, he heard the rattling of the cottage door and a tapping at the window; when the fisherman looked out of the window, he was face to face with a grey-bearded sailor in a cap and brass-buttoned jacket. The fisherman opened the door and went outside, but there was no one in sight!

A piece of driftwood found on the sands was sent to Edinburgh for examination, and the figure of a ghostly sailor was seen where ever the piece of driftwood was. Another local legend is of a Polish sailing ship driven ashore in the 1700s in Sandwood Bay, with loss of life to the crew. One headless crewmember is reported to be searching for his lost mate, or perhaps his lost head. (Courtesy of Peter Underwood and others)

Military Ghosts and Legends

The Bronze Age Warrior and Other Early Ghosts

The ancient counties of Dorset and Wiltshire are known as The Cradle of Civilisation in England. The Bronze Age (1900-500 BC) gives rise to the oldest-known warrior horseman ghost, who rides along the A3081 between Sixpenny Handley and Cranborne, Dorset, where it crosses the ancient earthwork called the Cursus, which consists of two parallel banks and ditches that run for 6 miles from Badbury to Salisbury. The whole area is covered with ancient burial barrows, Roman roads, earthworks and a fort at Penbury Knoll, near Bottlebush Down.

Over the centuries, local people are reported as having seen the ghostly warrior riding over Bottlebush Down. Two young local women, cycling at night from Handley to Cranborne, reported to the local Dorset Police Constable that they had been terrified by the sight of a man on horseback riding alongside them – but making no sound.

Substance was given to the reports in 1927, when a Dr R. C. Clay – an archaeologist of Fovant, Wiltshire – was driving along the A3081 one evening between Cranborne and Handley Cross when he saw the ghostly horseman riding bare-back on a small horse with a long mane and tail, but without stirrups or bridle, parallel to his car. The ghostly, bare-legged warrior was waving a sword with his right hand over his head, and was dressed in a roughly-woven, long, flowing, cloak-like garment. From the sword and garment, Dr Clay dated the ghostly figure as Late Bronze Age, some 700-600 BC. After a few moments, the spectral 3,000-year-old horseman disappeared near a low burial mound on Bottlebush Down. He was then seen at Squirrels Corner, emerging from another barrow. Dr Clay – who was working at an excavation at Christchurch – returned to Bottlebush Down the next day. His trained eye noted that there was a specific low burial mound, exactly where the ghostly rider had disappeared.

Burial barrows are thought to have 'Barrow guardians' who guard barrows, and it could be that the horseman of Bottlebush Down is one of them. Many locals have seen the ghostly horseman riding over the fields near the barrows.

At Kits Cory House, Aylesford, Kent, there is a megalithic barrow or burial place on Blue Bell Hill, where a British chieftain is reputed to be buried after he was killed in mortal combat with the Jutish leader Horsa in AD 455. His troops fought alongside him, and their ghosts are reported to be still fighting or re-enacting the battle of AD 455 – but in total silence. Pegwell Bay, Ebbsfleet, Kent, is where the invading forces of Hengist and Horsa landed in AD 449, and fought under a banner bearing a prancing white horse. Local legend has it that they still fight – again in silence.

Ghosts of the Battle of Nechtanesmere, Scotland

In May 685, the Battle of Nechtanesmere between the native Picts of Scotland and invading Angles occurred. The Picts, with their King Brude mac Beli, slaughtered the Angles led by their King Ecgfrith. Only a few Angles survived the massacre, located 8 miles from Letham, Fife, Scotland. The beaten Angles never returned to Scotland.

Nearly 1,265 years later, on 2 January 1950, a woman walking her dog on the snow-covered battlefield saw a ghostly repeat of the battle. She saw a mass of hand-held flaming torches held by seventh-century-clad Picts (who were identified by experts from their clothing), who were searching the bloody battlefield looking for their dead warriors to give them a Pictish funeral.

The Ghost of Finn McCoul and other Ghosts of Skye

On the moors near Loch Ashie, Inverness, witnesses state that they have seen, on May Day dawn, large bodies of ghostly men fighting on foot and horseback, killing each other with axe, sword and dagger. All in silence. Local folk tales say the Irish/Scottish folk hero Finn McCoul (Fionn mac Cumhail in Gaelic), wielding his great sword Mac a' Luin, fought a battle in ancient times to save Scotland from the Norse invaders. He, with his two great hounds Bran and Sceolang, and his followers, the Fianna foot soldiers, is said to be sleeping in underground caves on the island of Skye, waiting for their country to call them again to battle.

Also on the Isle of Skye, around Harta Corrie in Glen Sligachan, witnesses have seen large groups of silent, ghostly, kilted clansmen, reputed to be MacDonalds and MacLeods fighting a 300-year-old battle again and again, when the MacDonalds slaughtered the MacLeods. The actual scene of the battle in 1601 is marked by 'The Bloody Stone' at the entrance to the Corrie by the bed of the burn (stream). The MacDonalds cut off the heads of the MacLeods and rolled them down the hill into a loch; as the heads rolled downhill, they cried out 'We almost won today!' The loch is now known as the 'Loch of Heads'.

Headless ghosts abound in Skye; it seems to have been a clan custom of the islanders to cut off the heads of their enemies, with no quarter given. At Glashvin, on the beautiful Staffin Bay, a ghost known as 'The Headless Body' is said to carry his head under his armpit, and when he meets a victim, kills them by throwing his head at them.

Ghostly Roman Legions and Legionnaires

The Romans built upon an Iron Age hill-fort at Flowers Barrow, Worbarrow Bay, near Corfe, Dorset, and garrisoned it with a Legion of Roman soldiers. In December 1678, local people saw a ghostly column of several thousand Legionnaires marching along the Purbeck Ridgeway. The soldiers march along Bindon Hill, above Lulworth Cove; the noise of their marching is matched to that of horses being ridden, especially on foggy nights when their ghostly forms can be seen. The ghostly Legionnaires were seen just before the First World War broke out, and again in 1970. More Roman soldiers are said to march endlessly up and down Seacombe valley at Worth Matravers, Dorset. One column haunts the nearby cliffs.

The Romans fought a battle against the Britons at Bowerchalke, Wiltshire, and on moonlight nights, the battle is sometimes refought, with the clash of steel on steel and the tramping of Legionnaires. Legend has it that headless warhorses with unseen riders haunt Patty's Bottom, on one side of the village.

The ghost of a lone Roman soldier, dressed in leather armour, carrying a shield and wearing a helmet, haunts Thorncombe Wood, Bockhampton, Dorset. He walks and stands some 2 feet off the ground! This is due to his being on the site of a first-century AD Roman Road, which ran from Badbury Rings to Dorchester, which was higher then than the place where he is now seen. He was seen in late October 1969 by a group of people walking through the wood.

Roman soldier dressed for battle with lance (*pilum*), shield (*scutum*) and sword (*gladius*).

Richborough Castle, Kent. (*English Heritage*)

Richborough Castle, Sandwich, Kent, was a Roman Fort during the 500-year Roman occupation of England, and it is said that Roman soldiers who garrisoned the fort still march in and out.

Lympne Castle, near Hythe, Kent, has the ghost of a Roman soldier who fell to his death from a tower in the castle. Six other Saxon soldier ghosts are reputed to haunt the castle, the spirits of Saxons slaughtered by the invading Normans. At Slaybrook Corner, Hythe, Kent, a Roman soldier haunts the scene of an ancient battlefield there.

Near Wroxham Broad, Norfolk, a Roman soldier appears during March and October. He is then followed by a ghostly entourage of Roman gladiators, ready to do battle at the Roman Games which were once held here. At Wicken Fen, Cambridgeshire, a Roman army appears out of the fen then suddenly disappears. Ancient battles are heard but not seen in the area.

The cellars of the Treasurer's House (so named after previous occupants in 1539), once part of York Minster, York, Yorkshire, are haunted by a sixteen-strong troop of uniformed and armed Roman soldiers who emerge from a wall, preceded by an officer on a large horse, to the sound of a trumpet! They shuffle across the cellar floor in their issue leather boots, and disappear into the opposite wall! Many have witnessed the ghostly soldiers over many years. There is no noise of swords clashing on metal and leather armour creaking, no sound of horses' hoofs and no sounds of soldiers talking, as they did on a march. The soldiers are quaintly dressed in a uniform of rough, green-coloured cloth and splendid Roman plumed helmets. The trumpet, which heralds their arrival in the cellar, is a long, straight, heraldic type. The cellars were at one time part of a Roman road, which may account for the tramping soldiers and their leader on a horse using the ancient Roman road.

The invading Romans first arrived in the Peak District of Derbyshire in the latter part of the first century, and fought to subdue the ferocious Celtic Brigantes tribesmen; both sides gave no quarter. In an effort to colonise the district, two Roman forts were constructed at Brough near Bradwell, and Melandra in Glossop. A Roman road was constructed between the two forts, to try and keep the Brigantes under control by Roman soldiers marching along the road. There are persistent memories of a great battle between Romans and Celts in the High Peak District. Legend has it that hundreds of Celts were slain, and their bodies buried in barrows on Ludworth Moor, where they can still be seen. At different seasons of the year, when the moon is full, the ghosts of the Celts rise from their graves in the barrows and marshal on the battlefield, as if waiting for their ancient Roman foes. Phantom Legions of Roman soldiers still march across the ridge of hills between Hope and Glossop, and have been seen marching between the two Roman Forts at night, carrying flaming torches. Roman Legions are also seen on the A57 Snake Pass over the Pennines, usually on the time of the first full moon of spring, and have been described accurately by witnesses as to their shields, armour and weapons. (Courtesy of Dr Clarke)

The Thuringian Forest in Germany was the location of a ferocious no-quarter battle 2,000 years ago, between war-like German tribes and invading Roman soldiers. In the summer of 1887, a British Army officer was on a walking holiday in the Forest. Becoming tired, he sat down and rested by the roadway. Suddenly, to his amazement, he saw an entire Roman Legion marching by in step.

As an army officer who had studied military history, he was able to identify the ghostly Legion as about first century AD. Each legionnaire was clothed in thick leather, had upper body protection from a large rectangular *Scutum* (shield) and was carrying a sword (*Gladius*) on his belt. Each was armed with a small throwing lance (*pilum*), carried on the right shoulder.

As the officer watched, the Roman Legion gradually disappeared from his sight.

At Maumbury Rings, to the south of Dorchester, and on the Weymouth road, lies the ancient, oval-shaped Roman amphitheatre where Roman soldiers of Hadrian's Legions watched gladiators fight and die in mortal combat. The thirty-foot-high ramparts slope down to form a classic Roman arena. Local old Dorset people have said that they could often see ghostly combats, and hear the noise of steel clashing with steel and the roar of the crowds.

The Rings was also used in the eighteenth century as an ideal place for watching public hangings, and a gallows was placed in the centre of the arena. The public hangman carried out hangings, and the ghosts of those hanged still haunt the place of their execution.

The George and Dragon pub in Chester, Cheshire, was built on the site of a 1,600-year-old Roman cemetery. The popular pub has the ghost of a Roman centurion, who is still carrying out his watch-keeping duties by marching slowly and heavily over the pub's upper floors in the early morning. After an hour, the heavy tread is heard again; he passes through solid walls, and then there is silence.

Badbury Rings Slaughter

The ancient, fortified Celtic city lies just outside Wimborne, Dorset. The Romans, then the Saxons, occupied and enlarged the site.

In AD 520, the invading Saxons were encamped overnight in Badbury Rings when King Arthur's cavalry – who had ridden from Cadbury Camp, Somerset, some 25 miles away, overnight – attacked at daybreak, and slaughtered well over 1,000 Saxons. Romans haunt the Rings, and Saxon soldiers' ghosts, whom many visitors have seen. At Glastonbury, Somerset, the sounds of ghostly marching armoured soldiers have been heard.

A friend of the author – David Atfield – has seen a Roman soldier at the Rings. Oddly, the soldier, dressed in Roman leather battle armour, can only be seen from a certain angle and he never moves. As he is watched he fades away, but returns at intervals.

The Warrior Queen Boadicea's Ghost

Boadicea was the widow of the King of the Iceni, who occupied what are now Norfolk and Suffolk. She was a ferocious warrior, and gathered a large army round her. She and her army are said to have killed 70,000 of the invading Romans.

Boadicea, driving her two-horse chariot with knives on its wheels, fought the invading Romans until her followers and army were defeated in AD 62 by the Roman General Paulinus. To avoid capture and public execution by the invaders, the warrior Queen took poison and died. She is reputed to be buried under Platform Ten of what is now King's Cross railway station.

The Warrior Queen has been seen – usually in the morning – at the Lincolnshire village of Cammeringham, which is close to Ermine Street Roman Road. She drives her ghostly two-horse chariot with her long hair and clothing billowing in a ghostly wind. She is also reputed to haunt what is now Epping Forest with her daughters, near an ancient earthwork called Amesbury Banks. She is also reported as having been seen several times driving her chariot through a secret RAF nuclear bomb storage depot in East Anglia, followed by her men at arms behind her. (Courtesy of Martin Caiden)

King Arthur's Grave

The legendary King Arthur is reputed to have been buried at Glastonbury, sleeping until England needs his sword again. His believed remains were found in the twelfth century, together with a lead cross bearing the inscription 'Here in the Isle of Avalon the famous King Arthur is buried'. His bones were dug up and scattered in 1539, and legends and tales arose that his armoured knights march in the vicinity. On Midsummer's Eve every seven years, some believe that King Arthur and his knights, with flaming lances, emerge from Cadbury Camp – the believed site of Camelot – near Yeovil, to water their horses.

Glastonbury, Somerset. (*Iris Hardwick, courtesy Somerset County Council*)

According to legend, the knight Sir Bedivere flung King Arthur's magical sword Excalibur into Dozmary Pool, Bodmin Moor, Cornwall. The Pool, a mile in circumference, is said to be haunted by the ghost of an evil steward, magistrate, militia officer and murderer named Jan Tregeagle, who is condemned forever to empty the Pool with a limpet shell.

The Canvey Island Viking Ghost

Canvey Point, Essex, has the ghost of a Danish Viking warrior walking over the extensive mud flats of the Thames Estuary. It was here that a vicious battle was fought between the English and the Danish Vikings in 894. The Viking ghost is over 6 feet tall, and has a beard and long drooping moustaches. He wears the Viking horned battle helmet, and is armed with a two-handed, five-lobed long-sword (the term two-handed means the width of the grip – two hands are required to use it). Wearing a leather surcoat, he strides over the mud flats at night, leaving no footprints in the mud. Danish Vikings raided and fought against the Anglo-Saxons, and local legend has it that the Viking warrior ghost is looking for a Viking Longship to carry him home.

Canvey Island, site of the Viking ghost. (*Elli Constantatue, Essex County Council*)

The Vikings of Iona, Inner Hebrides, Scotland

The 3-mile-long by 1½-mile-wide ancient Isle of Iona was raided in 986 by Danish Vikings at White Sands, who slew the waiting – welcoming – monks, and set fire to the ancient abbey after robbing it of all valuables.

At White Sands in the north of Iona, a ghostly fleet of fourteen silent Viking longships laden with ferocious Norsemen has been seen re-enacting the raid of 986. As the witnesses watched in horror, the Norsemen landed and slaughtered the monks on the shore, then made for the abbey, seized the valuable property, and set fire – once again – to the ancient building. The Norsemen then loaded their long-ships with booty and rowed off out of sight along the Sound of Iona, towards the northwest, between the islands of Annraidh and Chalba.

King Edmund's Spurs

The Battle of Hoxne, Suffolk, was fought in 869, between the forces of Saint Edmund, the last King of East Anglia, and the invading Danes. Edmund was merely a boy, and not military-minded, but did wear a pair of golden spurs. He raised a local army of sorts, and took on the warlike Danes. The Danes routed Edmund's amateur army with ease, and the King fled for his life from the invaders.

When King Edmund reached the village of Hoxne, he hid under the river bridge. As he lay there in terror, a wedding party crossed the bridge en route to the local church, and as the party crossed, the bride cried out that she could see a pair of golden spurs glinting under the bridge. The Danes who found the terrified King Edmund heard the bride's cries; he was taken prisoner and tortured to make him worship Danish gods. Edmund refused, and was tied to a nearby oak tree and shot to death by arrows from Danish bowmen. Not satisfied with killing the King, the ferocious Danes cut off his head and threw it into a clump of gorse bushes.

Edmund's followers cut down his headless body, and reverently took it to the local church. Legend has it is that a ray of light came from the sky and illuminated the clump of gorse bushes. King Edmund's subjects searched the area lit up by the light from the sky, and found the decapitated head being guarded by a wolf.

The devout subjects built a chapel on the spot where the head was found, and it became famous for its power of healing the sick. With the passage of time, the chapel fell down and its location was lost. Many years later, a local lady found the location by seeing a ray of light from the sky falling on where the chapel had been. Professional archaeologists have uncovered the foundations of the long-lost chapel site.

Local legend has it that the gleam of King Edmund's golden spurs can sometimes still be seen in the moonlight under the bridge, which became known as Gold Bridge. The oak tree of death fell down in 1848, and in its wood was found one of the deadly Danish arrows that killed the King.

Dowsborough, Somerset, was the site of a Danish army camp where the ferocious soldiers ate, slept, and got drunk. Sometimes their drinking led to personal fights and killings. On storm-swept evenings and nights, the sound of their singing and fighting can still be heard.

Corfe Castle Ghosts

The 600-year-old Corfe Castle, Dorset, is now in ruins, but it has been used as a prison, fortress, and palace during its history. In 978, Ethelred the Unready's stepmother Elfrida, who wanted her son to occupy the throne of England, murdered King Edward the Martyr. Mysterious lights are said on occasion to light up the Castle ruins, and groans are heard coming from the castle's dungeon where French knights were imprisoned and left to die of starvation.

William the Conqueror – 1066

Ruined Pevensey Castle, Sussex, was the site of the first battle of the Norman Conqueror as he and his soldiers landed at Pevensey Bay in 1066. Local legends say that there is a ghostly horde of fighting men, led by William Rufus, tramping again and again from the sea over the marshes to the castle, where they vanish into the moat.

The great Battle Abbey, Sussex, built in 1070 on the site of the Norman victory over King Harold's Anglo-Saxons, has the mournful, bloodstained ghost of the King – with the fatal arrow through his eye – stalking the battlefield on the anniversary of his lost battle of 1066 when the Normans slaughtered the Anglo-Saxons. King Harold's body was recovered from the battlefield, and William had it buried under a pile of rocks on the nearby seashore. It was later removed and reburied in Waltham Abbey. All that now remains of the Abbey High Altar site is a fir tree.

St Nicholas' churchyard in Brighton, Sussex, has an ancient stone plinth, beneath which is said to be buried a knight and his horse, both wearing armour. A ghostly knight and horse emerge from the tomb and ride around the churchyard on moonlit nights. Sometimes the horse emerges on its own, and trots among the graves. Off Worthing Point every year, on 17 May, a ghostly sailing ship sails onto a hidden reef, which rips the bottom asunder, causing the vessel to heel over and sink in minutes with the loss of all hands and passengers on board. Fourteenth-century history has it that a Lord Manfred de Warrenne – who had been on a pilgrimage to Byzantium – was aboard and looking forward to being reunited with his betrothed (a Lady Edona), but drowned in the sea off Worthing, whilst his family and his betrothed watched in horror as the ship disappeared from sight under the waves. Manfred's father – the Earl de Warrenne – was overcome with grief at the death of his son and vowed to build a church in his memory. Accordingly, he built the Church of St Nicholas at Brighton.

The Ghost of Sir William Wallace

The ruins of the castle of the powerful Montgomery clan stands on what is known as Castle Hill, at Ardrossan, Ayrshire, Scotland, and is haunted by the ghost of the great Scottish patriot Sir William Wallace of Elderslie. After his defeat by Edward I in 1298 at Falkirk, Wallace was taken to England and drawn, hung and quartered on 23 August 1305, at Smithfield. His giant ghost has been seen on stormy nights in the castle ruins with his great sword raised in anger, still at battle with the English invaders.

The Battlefield of Neville's Cross Ghosts

The Battle of Neville's Cross, Durham (13 October 1346), was between the English and Scots, and proved a disaster for the invading 20,000-strong Scottish army under King David II. Opposing them at Neville's Cross was an English army some 15,000 in number, led by Lord Ralph Neville of Raby Castle, Durham. English archers and cavalry slaughtered the Scots without quarter. Their ghosts haunt the scene of their gory death. One of the dead soldiers' wives – carrying a baby – is believed to haunt the area of the battle, still looking for her soldier husband. In 1569, Charles Neville, Earl of Westmoreland, had Raby Castle as his stronghold, but was ill-advised to fight against the military power of Henry VIII. Neville fled abroad and was eventually buried in Holland, but his ghost returns to haunt what was his castle.

The Agincourt Funeral Procession

Sir Piers Leigh fought and died in battle at Agincourt in 1415, and his body was brought back to Lyme Park House, Disley, Cheshire. His sweetheart, Blanche, followed Sir Pier's funeral cortege though the Park, then died of a broken heart. Her ghost is said to haunt Lyme Park House, and her sad figure still follows his ghostly cortege, as it still sometimes winds its way through the Park.

The Ghost of the Black Prince

At Hall Place, Bexley, Kent, the ghost of the fourteenth-century Edward, the Black Prince of Wales (1330-1376), has been seen as a completely featureless black figure. The Black Prince commanded the vanguard at the Battle of Crécy in 1346, when he was but sixteen years of age, and for some unknown reason his ghostly appearance at Hall Place is said to presage great danger or warning to the British nation. During the First World War, his ghost was seen three times, each one before British defeats. He is often seen at dusk in his distinctive black armour, and to the strains of fourteenth-century music. The Black Prince of Wales is buried in Canterbury Cathedral, and his effigy in black armour is to be seen there.

Effigy of the Black Prince of Wales, Canterbury Cathedral. (*Canterbury Cathedral*)

The Rochester Castle Lady Ghost

On Good Friday, 1264, the castle was attacked by Simon de Montfort's troops, and one of the armed defenders was killed by an arrow through the heart – Lady Blanche De Warenne. Her alleged ghost, still with the arrow in her heart, revisits the Castle on the anniversary of her violent death.

Scottish and English Ghostly Soldiers

On 17 October 1346, the Scots, under King David Bruce, attacked Neville Castle, Durham, but were defeated, and the King was taken prisoner. Local legend has it that some people with sensitive minds can, if they walk round the castle nine times then lie on the ground, hear the sound of the battle.

The highways and byways around Market Bosworth, Leicester, are said to be haunted by the figure of a headless, ghostly soldier. No one knows who he is or when he died.

The Battle of Bramham Moor, near Tadcaster, West Yorkshire, took place in 1408, on the site of what is now Bramham Park. At night, the area of the cricket pitch resounds to the martial noise of ghostly men and horses, still fighting their long-ago battle. Other sounds are the panic-stricken soldiers fleeing the battlefield to save their lives – those soldiers who did not make it to safety and were slaughtered with no quarter given make the ghostly sounds.

The ruined Blanchminster Castle, Stratton, Cornwall, is haunted by a knight named Ranulph who went to the Crusades; when he returned, he found that his wife had remarried, thinking he was dead in battle against the Saracens. Ranulph was distraught, and became a hermit until his death. He was buried in the local church, but his ghost haunts the moat of his ruined castle. Nearby is the site of the Civil War Battle of Stratton, 16 May 1643, when a local army of Cornishmen killed over 300 of their enemy, and captured 1,500 soldiers. Some of the 300 dead are reputed to haunt the area of the battle.

The armour-clad ghost of Sir Robert Banastre, who died in the seventeenth century, haunts Passenham village, Northamptonshire. Shortly after his death, he appeared in full armour, walking the village streets and visiting houses. The local church sexton was digging Sir Robert's grave in the churchyard of St Guthlac's church, Passenham, when the ghostly knight appeared next to him, and said 'I am not yet ready'. The grave was filled in, but Sir Robert continued to stalk the village, saying 'Beware! Be Ready!' A local vicar performed a service of exorcism, during which Sir

Robert appeared in shining armour, begged the assembled village people to stop the service, and promised that he would stop haunting the village.

Kensington Palace is reputed to be haunted by the ghost of King George II, who looks out of a window. The legend is that he, as king and Commander in Chief of the Army and Navy, is looking for military despatches and letters from Hanover, Germany.

Blackness Castle, Blackness, West Lothian, was built in the fourteenth century, and rebuilt in the sixteenth century as an artillery fortress and armaments arsenal. The central tower is known as the Prison Tower from its incarceration of prisoners.

In 1998, a woman was climbing the dark, damp stairs of the grim Tower when a ghostly knight in full armour confronted her. Rooted to the spot, the woman was angrily berated by the ghostly knight, which forced her to run down the wet stairs and escape out into the courtyard. Strange noises, as if furniture was being moved bodily over a stone floor, have been heard, but nothing is seen.

The Slain Commander

During the Battle of Tewkesbury (4 May 1471), Lord John Wenlock was a Lancastrian Divisional Commander, directing the main battle under his Commander in Chief, the Duke of Somerset. The battle went badly for the Lancastrians, and the Duke of Beaufort is alleged to have beheaded Wenlock for failing to support him and changing side during the battle. The headless ghost of Lord John Wenlock is reputed to haunt the grounds of Someries House, Bedfordshire. A helmet said to be Wenlock's hangs in the church of St Mary, Luton, and Bedfordshire.

Ghostly Messengers

The village of Prestbury, Gloucester, is haunted by the ghost of a Royal Messenger riding a white horse at the gallop along Shaw Green Lane during the early hours of the day. Legend has it that he was a Royal Messenger galloping through the village in 1471, bound for the camp of Edward IV at Tewkesbury, when a well-directed arrow from the bow of a Lancastrian bowman killed him.

Also in Prestbury, during the English Civil War, Roundhead soldiers were encamped in the village. Fearing a night attack by Royalist cavalry, the resourceful troops stretched stout ropes at head height across the only road through the village. The trap worked when, one dark night, a

Royalist Messenger was caught by the rope and torn out of his saddle by the impact. He was put to the sword and died immediately, but his ghost is still riding with the King's messages.

His ghost and his ghostly horse are invisible, heard only as the pounding of hooves, which end abruptly at the spot where he met his death (The same method was used – successfully – during the Second World War by French resistance fighters during the German occupation, except they used wire!).

The Castle Ghosts

Ludlow Castle, Shropshire, has two ghosts. One is the Lady Marion de la Bruyere, who defended the castle in a siege. Unfortunately her treacherous swain was in the attacking force, so when she lowered a rope to admit him at night he left it there so that the attackers could gain armed access. The affronted Marion then slew her lover with his own sword, and committed suicide by jumping from the Hanging Tower. Her ghost still walks up the stairs of the Tower. The second ghost – a soldier – died in the castle around 1513, but for some reason he does not haunt the castle, but the nearby Globe Hotel.

The Crusader Ghost

Lacock Abbey, founded by Ela, Countess of Salisbury, stands in the meadows by the River Avon, Wiltshire. One night in 1250, the Abbess saw a ghostly, skeleton knight appear in her rooms in the Abbey. From the blazon of arms on his shield, she knew the knight was her son, who was fighting on Crusade in the Holy land. Six months later, news came from the Holy Land that her son, William Longspee, had died in battle with the Saracens, hacked to death by their deadly scimitar swords on the day that his ghostly figure appeared to his mother at Lacock.

The Edinburgh Mercat Cross Ghosts

The ancient Mercat Cross stands in Edinburgh, and it was here, the day before the Battle of Flodden, Branxton, Northumberland, on 9 September 1513, that ghostly men in unknown soldiers' uniforms appeared at the Cross and read out the names of all those Scottish soldiers who would die the next day in battle. The ghostly prophecy was correct, and the next day

Lacock Abbey.

10,000 Scotsmen and their King, James, died in battle with the English. They were the 'Flowers of the Forest', and a bagpipe lament is named after them.

Spanish Ghosts at Fort del Oro, Kerry, Ireland

In July 1579, King Charles V of Spain sent a punitive armed force to Ireland, which landed at Dingle Port, Kerry, Ireland. After a failed attempt at battle with local troops, the Spaniards built a stronghold at Ferrier Cove, and named it Fort del Oro.

In November 1580, the English sent an army and besieged the Fort, which held out for a time, but eventually they prevailed by force of arms. The Spaniards surrendered in good faith, but to no avail – the English soldiers massacred them by axe and sword to the last man. Their mutilated bodies were thrown into the sea or left where they were cut down. The Spanish soldiers' ghosts haunt the spot where they died in agony, and their Spanish voices are heard on the anniversary of their deaths, crying out in agony.

Major Weir's Ghost and the Devil

Thomas Weir, the devil's disciple, was born in Lanark, Scotland, in 1600. In 1649, he was appointed as Officer Commanding, Edinburgh City Guard. He supervised the execution of the Royalist Marquis of Montrose, and became a respected pillar of the Church. He bought a large house in

West Bow, Edinburgh, where he lived with his sister Grizel. In 1669, for some unknown reason, he confessed that he was in league with the Devil, and had for thirty-four years committed heinous sex crimes, with his sister Grizel assisting. He and his sister made full confessions of their crimes, which included necromancy and having a familiar spirit. She stated that the wooden staff carried by Weir was a gift from the Devil, and possessed strange powers. It could move of its own accord when directed by Major Weir.

Major Weir and his sister Grizel were arrested by the Civil Guard, and came to trial on 29 April 1670, where they were found guilty and sentenced to be executed. The unusual capital punishment handed down was to be strangled then burned. Major Weir was executed outside the City walls, and his staff was burned with him. His sister Grizel was hanged, burned, and then hung on a gibbet in Edinburgh's Grassmarket. Weir's house remained empty: no one would live in it for fear of the Devil, and the dark-cloaked ghost of Major Weir roaming the house and nearby streets, tapping the road with his magic staff. His sister Grizel, with her face and body badly burnt, is also seen there.

The Ghostly News Deliverer at Ballachulish, Argyllshire

Ballachulish House is the very ancient home of the Stewarts of Ballachulish. It was in this house, in 1692, that Captain Robert Campbell of Glenlyon received his orders to massacre all the MacDonalds under seventy at Glencoe. The Stewarts had no part in this treacherous breach of Highland hospitality, when a regiment of Campbells accepted Highland hospitality as guests, then killed thirty-eight of the sleeping Macdonalds in cold blood on 12 February 1692. The brutal atrocity known became as the Massacre of Glencoe. A ghostly horseman, clad in the tartan of the Stewart Clan, gallops to the main door of the House, dismounts and enters the door, then disappears. He is delivering the awful news of the Massacre of Glencoe to the Chief of the Clan Stewart. After the Massacre, ghostly pipers were said to lead the murdering regiment of Campbells astray in the wilds of Glencoe. Even today, Campbells are not welcome to the sad place of Glencoe. One pub even had a notice behind the bar, 'Nae Campbells served'. Perhaps in jest, but who knows?

In 1756, Colin Campbell, known as the Red Fox, of Barcaldine House, Glen Ure, was shot dead by an unknown assassin, and was laid to rest at Ardehatton Priory. A member of the Stewart Clan was accused of his murder and hanged at Ballachulish, but it was later found out that he was innocent of Campbell's murder. Campbell's restless ghost, dressed in Campbell tartan, walks the surrounding area of his death – still looking for his murderer, who was never found.

The Burnt Drummer

During the seventeenth-century Scottish Wars of the Covenanters, Lord Ogilvy's lookout drummer – a Cameron – was supposed to beat his drum as a warning when an enemy was approaching. When an enemy did approach Cortachy Castle – home of the Ogilvies – the drummer deliberately failed to give warning, and the enemy partly burned the castle. As a punishment, the defenders threw the treacherous drummer into the flames. His drum is said to be heard beating when an Ogilvy is about to die in the castle. In 1881, the ghostly drum was heard, and within an hour the death of the then Lord Airlie occurred. Another drummer at the castle was tied onto his drum and thrown off the high walls of the castle to his death – his drum is also said to be beaten by his ghost when one of the Airlie family is about to die.

Again, during the seventeenth century in Scotland, Royalist General Tam Dalyell (1599-1685) was reputed to be in league with the Devil, who promised him that he would be invulnerable in battle if he played cards with him and won. Dalyell's home was The Binns, Blackness, West Lothian, which he built to keep the Devil out. Dalyell, known as 'Bloody Tam', was invulnerable in battle, and ruthlessly slew his Covenanter enemies. Dalyell's playing cards, drinking goblet and knee-high riding boots are kept at The Binns. The riding boots are reputed to disappear when the ghost of General Dalyell borrows them to ride his horse around The Binns – still looking for enemy Covenanters.

Ghosts of the Civil War

The battles of the English Civil War gave rise to many ghostly tales and legends.

Sir Edmund Verney, the King's Standard Bearer at the first Battle of the Civil War – Edgehill, 23 October, 1642 – where he died clutching the King's Standard, haunts his old home Claydon House, Middle Claydon, Buckinghamshire. Sir Edmund's body was never found, but the King's Standard was recaptured from the Roundheads with his hand – severed by the Roundheads, who had tried to remove his dead fingers from the Standard, but could not do so – still clasping it. The hand still had Sir

Edmund's signet ring thereon, and was returned to Middle Claydon and buried, but ghostly Sir Edmund still mournfully looks for his severed hand. It is also said that his ghost appears whenever trouble threatens his country or family. Sir Edmund was one of the soldier ghosts who were recognised at the re-enactment of Edgehill at Christmas 1642, some months after the actual battle.

A 1,000-strong body of Roundheads led by a Major General Phillp Skippon besieged the Manor House at Grafton Regis, Northampton, on 21 December 1643. The Manor House was held and defended by Royalists under the command of Sir John Digby, who held out stoutly for four days until 24 December, when Sir John surrendered the Manor House to Major General Skippon. The next day, Skippon put the House to the torch to prevent it being used again as a Royalist base.

Three hundred years later – during the Second World War – on the same night as the House was first besieged on 21 December 1643, the local villagers were awakened by the sounds of battle coming from the site of the Manor House: the belching roar of cannon, cavalry riding at the gallop with the riders roaring out defiance at their enemies, the rattle of musket fire and the sound of sword blades clashing, and men dying in agony. Two ghostly armies were re-enacting their battle of the Civil War as the villagers cowered in their beds. The noise of battle continued on through the night until the late dawn, whereupon the noise died away.

Why did the ghostly armies wait three hundred years to re-fight their battle? Did the dramatic events of the Second World War, with the Allies beginning to gain the upper hand of the Germans, have anything to do with it?

Littledean Hall, Gloucester, has the ghosts of two Royalist officers who were murdered in the dining room. A ghostly bloodstain appears on the spot where they died. Both sides occupied the Hall during the Civil War! In 1740, two soldiers fought a duel in the grounds of the Hall – it is not known for what reason. Single-shot flintlock pistols were used, and the normal code of duelling, known as the Clonmel Rules, was adhered to. One man was killed, the other wounded. The dead duellist haunts the Hall, and is reputed to be looking for his wounded opponent.

The ghost of the Earl of Strafford haunts the Wheatsheaf Hotel, in Sheep Street, Daventry, and appeared as a ghost to Charles I when he slept there before the Battle of Naseby in 1645. The ghostly Strafford warned the King against battle with Cromwell's army, but Charles ignored the warning and lost the decisive Battle of Naseby. On Naseby battlefield itself, the local population have seen the battle re-enacted in the sky on its anniversary each year for over 100 years. A house at Callow End, near Worcester, has the ghost of a Cavalier who fought at the battle of Naseby.

The Boot Inn in Weymouth, Dorset was built around 1600, and is the oldest pub in the town. During the Civil War, a vicious, no-quarter battle took place outside the Inn between opposing Cavaliers and Roundheads. Many died in the slaughter, and five of their ghosts haunt the Boot Inn. The Inn is very popular despite the five ghosts, or perhaps because of them! And the beer is excellent, as the author can avow.

At Woodcroft Manor, Helpston, Huntingdonshire, the Civil War continues, with the ghostly sounds of steel on steel and the cries of the wounded and dying. The castle was the scene of a vicious no-quarter fight, when Cromwell's troopers slaughtered all the defenders to a man. The ghost of Charles I's chaplain, the Reverend Michael Hudson, is often seen and heard crying 'Mercy! Mercy!' He was thrown from the battlements, but managed to hold onto a projection. As he dangled there, trying to save his life, the soldiers cut off his hands, and he fell to his death.

Ghostly Battleground and Ghosts

The Wars of the Roses Battle of St Albans, Hertfordshire, took place in 1455, and on the anniversary of the vicious battle – 22 May – the buildings in Chequer Street which now occupy the space of the battlefield are said to be filled with the sounds of the battle – galloping horses and the clashing of swords – as ghostly armies clash, again and again. King Charles II used Salisbury Hall, near St Albans, as his headquarters. The ghost of one of his young Cavaliers haunts the Crown Chamber of the Hall, still with the sword that killed him protruding from his chest; his heavy footsteps are heard on the stairway. Legend has it that he was a Messenger to the King, and was on his way to the Hall when a party of enemy Roundheads waylaid him. Desperate to escape, as he knew he was facing certain death at the hands of the enemy, he made for the Hall and sought sanctuary, without result. In terror, he killed himself with his own sword. Those who have seen him describe him as young and handsome, and wearing classic Cavalier clothing and silver-buckled shoes. An armoured knight from the Middle Ages is often seen near the ancient bridge over the moat of the Hall.

Windmill House, Bishop's Stratford, Hertfordshire, has the ghost of a Volunteer Militia officer who was accidentally shot in the grounds of the House.

The Battle of Edgehill was fought on Sunday 23 October 1642, when two vast armies of Roundheads and Royalists, totalling some 26,000 fighting men, fought to a deathly stalemate draw. On Christmas Eve, 1642, three shepherds watching their flocks of sheep on the site of the Battle of

Edgehill, Warwickshire, saw the battle re-enacted in the sky above as a ghostly panorama of ghostly armies clashing in the sky for several nights. The shepherds reported the three-hour-long ghostly battle to their local clergyman, Samuel Marshall, and a local magistrate, William Wood, who promptly set off to report the matter to King Charles at Oxford.

Hearing of the hauntings, King Charles I sent a Royal Commission of officers under the leadership of Colonel Lewis Kirke, who had fought at Edgehill, to observe the unearthly battle, with Captain Dudley, Captain Wainman and three more officers. All on the Royal Commission had fought and survived Edgehill. After viewing several ghostly replays of the battle in the sky (each three-hour ghostly battle was bathed in a brilliant white light), the Commission reported back to Charles that on two occasions they had seen soldiers they had fought alongside fighting again in the sky. Statements were taken from local clergymen and magistrates – all respectable and men of substance – who had witnessed the ghostly battles.

In spite of the time elapsed since the Battle, there are still reports of it being refought again and again; now it appears to be only the noises of contempory war – shouts of the dying and wounded, the roar of gunfire and the clash of steel on steel A Royalist named Henry Kingsmill rode valiantly into the battle on a massive white horse and fought well and long, but the other side won and Kingsmill died in battle. The ghost of his white horse wanders the battlefield on each 23 October, looking for his master Colonel Kingsmill, who was buried at Radway, some short distance away. The Edgehill ghosts, incidentally, are the only ones which the Public Record Office accepts as authentic. In 1960, two soldiers posted to Melborough army camp near Edgehill arrived at the camp late one afternoon that winter, knowing nothing of Edgehill and its ghosts. During one spell of duty, the two soldiers heard screams and the sounds of battle. Scared to death, the two soldiers retreated to the guardroom and remained there for the rest of their spell of duty.

The site of the Battle of Marston Moor, on 2 July 1644, when Cromwell's 27,000 Roundheads defeated 18,000 Royalist Cavaliers at Long Marston, Yorkshire, is still haunted by the many spirits of 4,000 slaughtered Royalist soldiers who have been seen frequently in the area, fleeing to escape the Roundheads. One is said to be a headless Cavalier on horseback who appears to rise out of the ground of the battlefield when the nearby Long Marston village clock strikes the hour of midnight. He gallops for a mile then stops and waits, turns back, and gallops at speed back to where he emerged from and disappears slowly into the ground.

In November 1932, two men – Arthur Wright and a friend – were driving in a car across Marston Moor, when they had to slow their speed due to a dense fog. Suddenly, ahead of them, they saw in the car headlights a group of men dressed in Cavalier uniform, directly in their path The driver had to stop his car, and he and his passenger got out of the car to remonstrate with the group for standing in the roadway in a dense fog, but when they got out there was nothing – no Cavalier-dressed soldiers in sight. The road was empty. Reports of sightings have continued in 1968 and 1992.

At Wonson Manor, Gidleigh, on Dartmoor, four ghostly Cavaliers are sometimes seen seated around a table, playing cards with the owner of the manor who, eventually, after a run of bad cards, gambled away his manor.

Near Clovelly, in North Devon, stands Velly Farm, where it is said that another ghostly Cavalier haunts the cheese-making room at the back of the farmhouse. Also Castle Hill, Torrington, north Devon, is haunted by the ghost of a soldier killed in action at the Battle of Torrington, on 16 February 1646, during the Civil War. A Cavalier is said to haunt Downe Court, Orpington, Kent, and is reputed to appear in photographs taken on the stairs and library. At Salisbury Hall, Hertfordshire, the ghost of a Cavalier has been seen, still with the sword that killed him, thrust through his body by his own hands to avoid capture by pursing Roundheads. Woodham Ferrers, Essex, has the ghost of a Cavalier who haunts Edwin's Hall – the former home of Edwin Sandys, Archbishop of York in 1619. Another Cavalier haunts White Tyrells, also in Essex. Three bloodstained Cavaliers haunt the Chapel of the Great Hall of Gaulden Manor, Tolland, Somerset. They have been seen standing in front of the panelled walls. Cromwell's Roundheads were quartered at the Hall during the War.

At Poyntington, some 2 miles north of Sherborne, Dorset, lie the unmarked graves of badly-armed peasant Royalist supporters who were buried in the field by the stream where they fell in June 1644. Under the command of one twenty-year-old Baldwin Malet, the Royalists engaged Cromwell's troops, but in spite of Malet on his horse killing twenty Roundheads with his sword, they were slaughtered and beheaded to a man. Their restless ghosts still linger at night where they fell, near the grassy mounds of their graves, which can still be seen on the meadows near the millstream. Malet died of wounds, and was buried next day in the local churchyard, where a painting records his death. Reports tell of a small body of headless men and one headless woman – who she was, no one knows – haunting the area.

Wardour Castle, Ansty, Wiltshire (the home of the Arundell family), was built in 1392, but is now in ruins after being blown up during the Civil War. Lady Blanche Arundell, with twenty-five men, held the castle against the Roundheads for five days, then was granted honourable terms of surrender. The Puritans who slaughtered all of the defenders did not keep the surrender terms. The brave lady was buried at nearby Tisbury. Her ghost is said to haunt the area near the castle lake.

Arundel Castle, since 1580 home of the Dukes of Norfolk, who are the Earls Marshal of England, was bombarded and battered by Cromwell's guns under the direction of Sir William Waller. Some say they can still hear the roar and boom of the cannon on occasion. In the huge library of the castle, the ghost of a Cavalier has been seen since the time of Charles II – he has been named the Blue Man of the library, as he wears a blue silk Cavalier suit, and sits reading books from the shelves of the library. At Crondall, Hampshire, the ghosts of Cromwell's mounted troops still ride along the road to the church.

During the Civil War, Sir Robert Pye was on the Roundhead side, but his father was a Royalist who held the family home – Faringdon House, Berkshire – for the King. Sir Robert attacked Faringdon House, but was killed. His headless ghost haunts Faringdon church. The churchyard at Faringdon, Berkshire, is also reputed to be haunted by the ghost of an eighteenth-century naval officer, Hampden Pye, who was murdered by arrangement. Pye's stepmother paid his captain to arrange for the ship's gunner to blow his head off during a sea battle. The murder was duly carried out, and Pye's head blown off. Pye's headless ghost returned to haunt his captain and his stepmother by riding with her in her coach – and the gunner who had blown his head off.

The headless ghost of a Cavalier named Goring rides a white horse each 15 June from High Down House, Pirton, Hertfordshire, some 3 miles to Hitchin. Goring had hidden in a hollow elm tree, but was found and killed instantly by searching Roundheads as his future wife watched from a window in horror. Another ghostly cavalier rides the road from Ingatestone to Stock, Essex.

Newton le Willows, Lancashire, is said to echo each August to the shuffling footsteps of Royalists and Highlanders making their way to be hanged. They were captured by Cromwell's troops, and hanged in August 1648 from tree branches.

Woodstock Manor, Woodstock, Oxfordshire, once stood in the grounds of Blenheim Palace Park, and was occupied by Cromwell's Commissioners from 13 October to 2 November 1649. A ghost known as the 'Royalist Devil of Woodstock', who caused mayhem to all therein, plagued them. Glass was broken and thrown about, candles mysteriously went out, and urine from chamber pots was thrown over beds. The Commissioners gave up and moved out; 'The Royalist Devil' also moved out, and has not been heard of since. The site is now a ruin, with only a stone marking where it once stood.

After the Battle of Pitreavie in 1651, Cromwell's Roundheads quartered themselves at Fordell, Fife. The Fordell miller had several platoons of troops quartered at his mill who, like victorious soldiers worldwide in those times, raped his wife and daughter continually. The enraged miller poisoned the Roundhead troops, who all died in agony. A squad of Roundheads came to the mill to hang the miller, but he had fled the scene. The Roundheads, unable to exact revenge on the miller, hanged his apprentice Jock instead on a nearby tree. Local stories tell that on occasions Jock can be seen still hanging from the old tree, his contorted face and bulging eyes clearly visible on moonlit nights.

The ghost of Lord Holland, executed during the Civil War, during which he was a Cavalier, haunts Holland House, Westminster, London. The House is now an International Youth Hostel much used by foreign students, and Holland's ghost has been seen by some of them.

Watton Abbey, Yorkshire, has the ghost of a cavalier standing by the fireplace in a bedroom which was used by Royalists during the Civil War.

Cromwell's Ghost

The ghost of Cromwell himself is said to haunt The Old Hall in the village of Long Marston – The Old Hall was his HQ during the Battle of Marston Moor. Cromwell, dressed in armour, appeared again in 1832 at Apsley House, London, home of the Duke of Wellington. He is also said to haunt the Golden Lion Inn, St Ives, Huntingdon, and the tithe barn at Plover's Dell, Hampshire. In London, Red Lion Square is one of his appearance sites, along with two other men, said to be Ireton and Bradshaw, who signed the death warrant of Charles I.

The Ghostly Cavalier

The Crab and Lobster public house at Siddlesham, 5 miles south of Chichester, Sussex, stands on the site of an old Inn, and is reputed to be the haunt of five escaping Cavaliers, among them Sir Edward Earnley, who fought a pistol battle with Cromwell's troopers outside the Inn. The troopers shot down all five Cavaliers, and then carried them into the Inn to die. Since then, it is alleged that the figure of a tall, cloaked man has been seen in the present bar of the pub. During the summer of 1969, a medium visited the Crab and Lobster for dinner, and stated that she had seen the figure of a Cavalier lying on the bar floor, dying from a bullet wound to the chest. (Courtesy of Peter Underwood)

Rebellious Ghosts

Sedgemoor, Weston Zoyland, Somerset, is the location of the last battle fought on English soil, early on 6 July 1685, when James Scott, Duke of Monmouth (1649-85), the illegitimate son of Charles II, landed at Lyme's Cobb, Dorset, then led a rebellion of peasant soldiers against the troops of the King James II to claim the throne.

Monmouth stayed overnight at the Great House, (Raynham Hall), Norfolk, and his ghost haunts a room now known as the Monmouth Room. He appears, not as an ordinary Cavalier, but as the dashing Red Cavalier, with a reputed eye for the ladies. He appears if a lady sleeps in the bed, and she usually awakes to see him smiling and bowing with his plumed hat sweeping the floor in a gallant gesture of greeting.

The Duke of Monmouth fled from the Sedgemoor battlefield, but was captured by enemy soldiers early on the morning of 7 July 1685, at Horton Heath, near the village of Woodyates, which lies on the site of the old Roman road which ran from Badbury Rings, Dorset, to Salisbury. He is reputed to have lodged at the Woodyates Inn on the night of 6 July 1685.

The defeated Duke of Monmouth was beheaded on 15 July at Tower Hill, London, by bungling executioner Jack Ketch, who took eight strokes of the axe to behead the Duke. His peasant troops were butchered; their ghosts (said to number over 1,000) still linger on the site – some reported as balls (orbs) of light. The dead of both sides were buried on the battlefield. Monmouth's bewigged and cloaked ghost has been seen at the Woodyates Inn on the 15 July of each year. He is also seen, annually on 7 July, around midnight, on a white horse, trotting sedately along on the A3070 road from Uplyme to Yawl, Devon. At this location he is reported as having his head on.

On 6 July each year, the ghostly figure of the Duke of Monmouth on horseback rides the battlefield, still escaping in blind panic, vainly riding eastwards to safety. He was seen on horseback in July 1912, and identified as Monmouth, dressed in a cloak, broad-brimmed hat and high riding boots. Ghostly horsemen, troopers and the peasant army still flee from the wrath of the King along the paths and roads around Sedgemoor. Walkers on the riverbank by the River Cary have heard ghostly voices, asking them to 'Come on over and fight'.

On the night of 6 July 1944, Trevor J. Kenward, a Council member of the Ghost Club Society, arranged an all-night vigil at the actual battle site. All the odd happenings were recorded in their log-book during the vigil: there were sounds like musket shots, drum beats, the pounding of horses' hoofs, all part of a ghostly battle. At one time, the ground vibrated for almost three minutes. All the sounds were recorded on tape recorders

– one member of the group felt a definite feeling of unease and evil that lasted for twenty-five minutes. (Courtesy of Peter Underwood)

The King sent the notorious Judge Jeffries to the West Country to mete out retribution, and over 200 of Monmouth's men were hanged. The branches of Heddon Oak, Crowcombe, some 50 miles west of Sedgemoor battlefield, were used as a gallows, and the sounds of ghostly men in chains choking out their lives on the gallows rope has been heard. Villagers say that they have felt a strangling sensation in their throats when they pass the site, and the sound of hoof beats and running feet.

Taunton Castle was Judge Jeffries' Taunton Assize Courtroom, in what was the Great Hall of the castle, which is now reputed to be in the Castle Hotel. The corridors of what was Taunton Castle are said to echo to the heavy-footed sounds of the Royalist troops dragging their peasant prisoners to death. The ghostly figure of a soldier wearing a sword and carrying a flintlock pistol in his hand has been seen on a stairway and landing. A female ghostly violin player has been seen in a Civil War evening dress gown. Also at Taunton, the Tudor Inn is reputed to be the setting of Jeffries' Courtroom, but also claims to have the bedroom in which he slept. Running alongside the Inn is Hangman's Walk, a very old flagstoned pathway. This was the path used by the public hangman, who hanged prisoners after Judge Jeffries had found them guilty and sentenced them to death.

Lyme Regis, Dorset, has the ghost of Judge Jeffries haunting Broad Street, where the Great House once stood, and where twelve Lyme Regis peasant soldiers hanged after being found guilty by Judge Jeffries of assisting Monmouth in his rebellion. The ghostly Judge is said to gnaw a bloody human limb as he walks Broad Street. The Hanging Judge, as Jeffries was known, also haunts Lydford in Devon.

The ghost of Charles I frequents Marple Hall, Cheshire, which was owned by Henry Bradshaw, whose brother John Bradshaw signed the death warrant of Charles I. Another story is that he lodged at a house in Churchyard Field, Catcott, Bridgewater, Somerset, on the night before the battle and haunts the area, but has no head. Some have it the headless ghost seen is that of the Duke of Monmouth.

The seventeenth-century Bywater House, Boldre, Hampshire, was haunted by the ghost of a young soldier who was killed there in 1685 whilst carrying secret despatches for the Duke of Monmouth, who had just been defeated at the Battle of Sedgemoor. He was buried in the garden of the House, and when a photograph of the garden was taken in 1920, it showed the figure of a young soldier in Cavalier dress with fair, curly hair standing by his grave.

The Ghostly Lovers on Horseback

Goodrich Castle, Goodrich, Herefordshire, stands on the River Wye, some 4 miles north-west of Monmouth. During the Civil War, it was a bastion of the Royalist cause. Parliamentary troops set the castle under siege, bombarding it with 250-lb cannonballs fired from a mortar. The mortar was angled to ensure that cannonballs fell on the inside of the castle, as well as breaching the massive walls.

Two young lovers – Alice Birch, and a Royalist officer, Charles Clifford – were trapped inside the castle and determined to make an escape from the imminent destruction of the castle. Waiting until darkness fell, Charles Clifford mounted his horse and lifted Alice up beside him. The drawbridge was lifted for the two lovers to escape over, and Clifford gave his mount its head. Crashing through the sleeping Roundheads, Clifford made for the River Wye.

The River Wye was in flood, and as the two attempted to cross on horseback, the surging current took the horse's feet away and the two lovers were swept downstream to their deaths. Their ghosts haunt Castle Goodrich, and they are also seen on horseback entering the River Wye, still trying to escape on horseback when the Wye is in flood.

Ghostly Hooves and Running Feet

Near Weston Zoyland, Somerset, locals say that the ghostly sound of horse's hooves, human panting, and running feet can be heard, the legend being that one of Monmouth's soldiers – a big, strong, fit man – was captured by King James's soldiers, and told that if he could outrun a horse he could live. The soldier outran the horse, but his captors still killed him. He is said to still outrun the horse as he haunts the location of his death.

Ghostly Locking Manor House Owners, and other Ghosts in Somerset

At Locking Manor, Somerset, the ghosts of Sir John Plumley and his wife haunt the manor house, walking with their dog. Sir John supported Monmouth, but after the disaster at Sedgemoor returned to his own manor house where he hid, but was inadvertently betrayed by his dog. He was hanged on an elm tree, and his wife committed suicide by drowning in Locking Well with their dog in her arms. Sir John has been seen with his dog, also with his wife and dog, near the yew trees near the manor drive; then they disappear into a disused well.

Curry Mallet Manor House, Somerset. (*Somerset County Council*)

The banqueting hall of the manor house at Curry Mallet, near Taunton, echoes to the sounds of sword on sword, wielded by unseen hands. Footsteps have been heard going up and down, to and from the Minstrel's gallery, but there is no visible presence. In the grounds outside there are many more ghosts, but it is not known who or why they are there.

The A30 main road from Crewkerne to Chard is believed to be haunted by those locals who use it. The sounds of ghostly galloping horses are heard, then the sounds of pistol shots, and the clash of steel on steel cutlasses. Local legend has it that there was an affray between brandy and silk smugglers and the king's customs officers, in which blood was drawn. One of the customs officers was badly wounded and died; the sounds of his dying throes are often heard.

The Ghostly Army

On the summit of Conygar Hill, a few miles from Dunster, Somerset, stands Luttrell's Folly: a round, turreted structure built by the local family of Luttrell *c.* 1760, and about 23 miles from Sedgemoor. During the Civil War, Monmouth's peasant troops marched across the West Country, and the Castle at Dunster was held by both sides during the war.

During the hot summer of 1951, two ladies climbed the steep sides of Conygar Hill and went into the Folly. In spite of the hot, sunny, windless

Luttrell's Folly, built *c.* 1760, Dunster, Somerset. (*Iris Hardwick, courtesy Somerset County Council*)

day outside, the ladies felt the temperature drop and the sunlight dim. Suddenly, they heard the sound of soldiers marching in step and coming towards them from the north – but they saw nothing except the tree on the hill swaying in a sudden wind. Frightened by the sound of the marching men, the two women ran down the steep hillside, away from the Folly. When they reached the bottom and looked back, there was no wind and no sound of marching feet.

The Pub Ghost

Norton St Phillip, Frome, Somerset, has the 300-year-old Fleur de Lys pub on the corner of the main road thorough the village. The Duke of Monmouth's rebel soldiers (in reality peasants) who supported his uprising were caught as they fled to their homes, tried after a fashion, then led to their execution to a field behind the Fleur de Lys pub. An innocent traveller in the pub was caught up in the hasty procession of condemned men. Despite his protestations, he was hanged with the rest of the peasants. His aggrieved ghost is said to still haunt the ancient pub with clanking chains – but as he was led to his death he was not in chains!

The Headless Spanish Soldier

The aim of the first Jacobite rebellion of 1715-1719 was to place the Old Pretender – the titular King James VIII of Scotland and King James III of England – on the English throne. To help James VIII's cause, Cardinal Alberoni of Cadiz sent 300 Spanish soldiers to fight for James VIII. The 300 Spaniards landed from two frigates in Loch Aish.

The ancient Eilean Donan castle, built in 1220 by King Alexander II of Scotland, stands on the Kyle (Strait) of Lochalsh, at Dornie, on Loch Aish. Some 300 Spanish soldiers were garrisoned at Eilean Donan Castle, home of the Earls of Seaforth – the remnants of the body of Spaniards who took part in the Battle of Glen Shiel on 11 June 1719, where they had to surrender when attacked by Hanoverian Government troops armed with four field mortars. The Hanoverians then bombarded Eilean Donan Castle from the sea with the guns of three frigates and the four mortars of the ground troops. The castle was reduced to ruins; many of the Spanish troops were killed in the action. One, who was killed when his head was blown off by artillery fire, haunts Eilean Donan Castle, carrying his head under his arm.

Ghosts of the Battle of Killiecrankie

The Pass of Killiecrankie ('Wood of Aspens' in Gaelic) was the scene of the vicious no-quarter Battle of Killicrankie on 27 July 1689, between Jacobite Highlanders loyal to the deposed King James II led by Viscount John Graham of Claverhouse ('Bonnie Dundee'), and forces loyal to William of Orange, led by General Hugh Mackay of Scourie. Graham had 2,500 Highlanders, and Mackay 3,400 troops.

The site of the battle was heavily wooded, with the River Garry on one side and steep hills on the other. The Highlanders were on their home ground, and used to mountain warfare. The other side was not versed in such warfare.

Mackay exhorted his troops – the East Yorkshire, King's Own Scottish Borderers, Scots Fusiliers, and the Royal Irish, with the Somerset Light Infantry in reserve – to stand fast and use their single-shot flintlock muskets and fixed bayonets to best advantage.

At about 7.00 p.m., in the red glow of a summer evening, the Jacobites unleashed the famous ferocious Highland charge. Naked and shoeless, dressed only in their weapons – muskets, pistols, broadsword, targe (shield) and dirk – the Highlanders shot and cut Mackay's army to pieces with their broadswords. But three volleys of musket fire from Mackay's

The Pass of Killiecrankie. (*Peter Underwood and the Scottish Tourist Board*)

troops killed John Graham and 900 of his Highlanders. John Graham was supposed to be a warlock, and legend has it that a silver musket ball killed him. A friend of Graham was Lord Balcarres of Colinsburg Castle, who was prevented by the Scottish Parliament from joining his friend in battle by being put under house arrest. The morning after the battle, Balcarres awoke and saw John Graham standing by his bedside, gazing down at him. Not knowing that Graham had been killed the day before, Balcarres spoke his apology to the ghost – who abruptly disappeared.

Since the battle, the ghosts of dead Highlanders and soldiers haunt the Pass of Killiecrankie. A red glow bathes the Pass on the anniversary of the battle. In the gloaming (twilight), ghostly troops and Highlanders march and charge in re-enactment of the slaughter. Flintlock musket fire can be heard, firing in volley, and ghostly dead bodies have been seen, lying where they fell and died.

The Black Colonel's Ghost

After the battle of Killiecrankie, Royalist soldiers demolished Colonel John Farquharson's Inverey Castle. Before he died, the Colonel, known as 'The Black Colonel', said he wished to be buried in the grounds of his Castle. However, he was buried in St Andrew's Churchyard in Braemar, Aberdeenshire. But his spirit did not want to be there! The day after his funeral, his coffin was found on the ground beside his grave. The coffin was buried three more times, but each time it re-appeared above ground! The mourners then remembered that he had wished to be buried at Inverey, and they carried out his wishes. Many years later, his grave was broken into and two men took one of his teeth each from his skull. The same night, the Colonel's ghost appeared to the two men and ordered them to replace his teeth by nightfall of the following day. The teeth were returned to the grave during the day. The Black Colonel was satisfied that he was at Inverey with his teeth restored, and there were no more sightings of his ghost. (Courtesy of Peter Underwood)

The Ghostly Colonel

In 1770, the Squire of The Old Hall at Ranworth, Norfolk, Colonel Thomas Sidney, took part in a two-man horse race with a neighbour. The neighbour was winning the race, but the jealous Colonel shot his horse from under him, causing the neighbour fatal injuries. Legend has it that the same night the Devil came for the Colonel and took him away on horseback. Each 31 December, the ghostly Colonel re-appears at the scene.

The Dragoon Trumpet-Major's Hand

On the night of 16 December 1780, a Dragoon Trumpet-Major named Blandford was illegally poaching deer with seven cronies on Chettle Common, Cranborne Chase, Dorset. Five local gamekeepers caught them in the act. A fierce sword and pistol fight ensued with the gamekeepers, in which Blandford's hand was cut off by a keeper's sword and fell to the ground. One of the gamekeepers died in the affray.

Trumpet-Major Blandford eluded the gamekeepers and made post haste for London, but left his hand behind. The gamekeepers found the hand, and had it buried in a churchyard with full military honours at Pimperne village, just outside the market town of Blandford, Dorset. The buried hand is said to be looking for its Trumpet-Major owner, and haunts the locality trying to find him.

Major Blandford was captured later with the remaining members of his gang, and sentenced to seven years transportation, later reduced to imprisonment in Dorchester Prison. Trumpet-Major Blandford later died in London, but it is said that his ghost still returns to Pimperne churchyard searching for his lost hand, in what is known as Bussey Stool Walk.

The Drummer's Revenge

The 4,500-year-old Stonehenge circle stands on the bleak Salisbury Plain – a cold, forbidding place in winter. Local people know it as 'The Stones'. During a violent night-time electrical storm which raged over the ancient stones in 1786, a sailor named Gervaise Matcham was walking past 'The Stones' with a sailor companion, when he saw the ghostly figure of a drummer boy coming silently towards them. Stricken with terror, Matcham confessed to his companion that he had murdered the drummer in 1780 at Brampton, Huntingdonshire. The companion reported the crime to the authorities, and Matcham was tried, then hanged at Huntingdon and hung on a gibbet. As he went to the gallows, it is said that the ghostly drummer boy accompanied him on his last journey. Matcham's body hung on the gibbet cage for many years. It is said that the drummer boy still marches past Stonehenge.

Stonehenge, Wiltshire. This photo was taken by the author in 1948, before the public were excluded.

The Deadly Duel

Two officers of the 46th Regiment of Foot (The King's Own Yorkshire Light Infantry), Surgeon George Crigan and Lieutenant Colonel Bryan Bell, fought a sword duel on the banks of the River Ouse at Fulford, Yorkshire, on 11 June 1797. The experienced Colonel had the better of the bitter fight (no one seems to know the reason for the duel), and killed the Surgeon by running him through with his sword. The Colonel and his two seconds were arrested, and imprisoned in York Castle for murder. However, the murder charge was reduced to manslaughter, and the Colonel was sent to prison for only a month!

The ghost of the dead Regimental Surgeon soon began to appear at the site of the duel, and did so until the location was made a tarmac roadway.

The American Major-General Ghost

Major-General Anthony Wayne was a famous soldier in the American War of Independence, renowned for his courage, dash and valour in battle. He died on 15 December 1796, and was buried in his native Pennsylvania.

His ghost haunts the battlefield of Brandywine, Pennsylvania where, in September 1777, he and his soldiers fought a stubborn rearguard action against the British army at Chadd's Ford. Wayne's ghost, dressed in cavalry dress, and riding his favourite white horse, Nab, thunders along the roadway by the battlefield, just as he did when resisting the British Army during his epic rearguard action.

Wayne has also been seen, wearing Indian, not Army dress, at Lake Memphremagog, at a lakeside log-fort used by fur traders, and also at Fort Ticonderoga, which he commanded in 1771. Riding his horse, the Major-General rides along Storm King Pass on the Hudson River at midnight, in a re-enactment of his ride of 1779, when he warned American forces against attack by British forces.

The Faithful Drummer Boy

During the harsh February of 1815, an army drummer boy returned home on leave to Potter Heigham, Norfolk. There he met a local girl, and they fell in love, but the girl's father refused to allow her to marry. The two lovers met secretly at the ice-covered Hickling Broad, and each time the drummer boy skated over the ice to meet his secret love.

One evening, the ice could not bear the weight of the drummer boy, and he fell through to his death in the icy water. Over the years since his death, the roll of a drum can be heard at 7.00 p.m. over Hickling Broad on a cold February evening – the ghostly drummer boy is still skating over the ice-covered Broad to meet his sweetheart.

The Headless Drummer Boy and other Ghosts

The ghost of a small, headless drummer boy, murdered at Dover Castle, Kent, during the Wars against Napoleon, marches around the castle still sounding his drum. Another small, headless, drummer boy drifts soundlessly through Edinburgh Castle, Scotland.

During the eighteenth century, it was customary to enlist Negroes in British regiments as trumpeters or drummers; for example, in 1759 the Life Guards had a Negro trumpeter. At Winchelsea, Sussex, the red-uniformed figure of a Negro haunts the churchyard.

Hurstmonceaux Castle, Eastbourne, Sussex, (now the Royal Observatory) was built by Sir Roger de Fiennes in 1440. It is reputed to have many ghosts, but the most fearsome is the Giant Drummer, servant of Sir Roger Fiennes, who marches round a room known as the Drummer's Hall and round the castle walls with his glowing drumsticks, beating out an insistent call.

Dover Castle, Kent. (*English Heritage*)

The ancient Edinburgh Castle dates from Pictish times, and has seen military service since the seventh century; it is still partly occupied by the military now. It has several ghosts, and on one occasion when one appeared, a sentry collapsed with fright. Home of the world-famous Edinburgh Military Tattoo with its blazing cressets (beacons), and with scores of drummers playing, it is perhaps fitting that one ghost is that of a headless drummer boy who has been seen in different part of the castle. No one seems to know who he is, but he plays well then disappears in a drifting, wraith-like manner.

Thomas, or Tobias, Gill – a Negro drummer of Dragoons – raped then murdered a young country girl at Blythburgh, Suffolk, in the mid-1700s. Gill was captured and hanged from a local tree on a crossroads in Toby's walk. Local legend alleges that a ghostly black coach with four headless horses, driven by Gill, careers silently down the lane where he was hanged.

The Ghostly Drummer and other Ghosts of Tedworth (Tidworth)

In April 1661, it was reported that a ghostly drummer dressed in a soldier's uniform was haunting the roads around Tidworth House, South Tidworth,

Hampshire, and Wiltshire. All who heard the sound of his ghostly drum were compelled to dance until they collapsed or the drummer stopped his insistent beat. At North Tidworth army camp, Wiltshire, a ghostly Roman soldier dressed in leather armour and carrying a *gladius* sword has been seen frequently. A ghostly, tartan-kilted soldier strides purposefully across the army rifle range at Tidworth – no one knows which regiment or army unit he served with. As he is wearing a tartan kilt, it must have been a Scottish one.

The Bedfordshire Militia Ghost

To the west of Daventry, Warwickshire, lies Shuckburgh Hall, where the ghost of a Lieutenant Sharp of the Bedfordshire Militia walks with his lady. The Lord of the Manor, Sir Stewkly Shuckburgh, did not approve of the soldier laying suit to his daughter, and the despairing Lieutenant shot his love, then himself, rather than give her up.

Demon and Ghostly Pipers

The pipe is one of the most ancient of musical instruments, and when attached to a bag it becomes a bagpipe. The Great Highland Bagpipe is principally a war pipe, and can be heard over a distance of up to 10 miles. The Duke of Sutherland has a bagpipe which can be heard at a distance of 8 miles. In Scottish superstition, this fearsome instrument is reputed to be the 'Devil's Favourite'. During the First World War, the German Army regarded the bagpipe, and kilted soldiers charging with the bayonet, as the Devil's own, and the soldiers as the 'Ladies from Hell'. This was, and probably still is, the ferocious Highland Charge of Scottish soldiers. Scotland is riddled with tales of the Devil appearing and playing the Bagpipes.

The Headless and other Pipers and Ghosts

An unknown ghostly headless piper can be heard on occasion, playing a wild rant of the pipes on Corsock Hill, north east of Dumfries, Scotland. Another ghostly piper plays on Piper's Brae, near Culzean Castle, Wigtownshire. He is reputed to be the ghost of the Clan Kennedy piper.

The ghost of Bonny Prince Charlie haunts the County Hotel in Dumfries, where he stayed in 1745. The room in which he slept is much as it was, but now has been carpeted in Prince Charles Edward Stuart tartan. (Courtesy of Peter Underwood)

The site of a Dumfries friary church is haunted by the ghosts of Robert the Bruce and the Red Comyn – rivals for the Scottish throne. In 1306, to gain the throne of Scotland, The Bruce stabbed the Red Comyn on the altar, and put his boot on the dying man to hold him down, saying 'Mak siccar' (Make sure), till Comyn was dead. Bruce is reputed to haunt a cave on Rathlin Island, County Antrim, near the lighthouse. This is where he had his famous encounter with the spider that he saw try and try again to spin a web. The spider eventually succeeded, and Bruce took it as a sign that he should try again and take the crown of Scotland. He did, and succeeded!

Yet another ghostly piper plays in the tower of Duntrune Castle, on the shores of Loch Crinan, Argyll. The castle was, until 1729, the home of the Campbells of Duntrune, but was for a brief time captured by the fearsome MacDonalds. The Campbells retook the castle and killed all within, except for the Macdonald's piper – it was bad luck to kill a piper.

The MacDonalds, under Chief MacDonald Coll Ciotach, began to launch another attack on the Campbell castle, but the spared MacDonald piper gave warning of the waiting Campbells to the approaching MacDonalds by playing 'The Piper's Warning to his Master'. The approaching MacDonalds heeded the piper's warning, and they retreated. In revenge, the Campbells cut off the piper's hands.

During the following years, the sound of the piper playing his warning went through the castle until early in the 1900s: during rebuilding work, two severed hands were found under the kitchen floor and a handless skeleton was found bricked up behind a wall. The remains were given a Christian burial – the piper was heard no more.

In the year 1700, a resident of Glasgow was passing through a local kirkyard when he saw the ghost of one of his recently-deceased friends rise out of a grave to the wild rant of bagpipes being played by the Devil! The horrified resident took to his heels, and reported the happening next day to his Minister.

At Gight Castle, Methlick, Aberdeenshire, a ghostly piper plays laments. The legend is that the piper was ordered by the Laird of the castle to walk through an underground tunnel leading from the castle to the grounds, playing his pipes as he did so. The piper entered the tunnel from the castle, but he was never seen again.

Clan Chattan's Chanter

The ancient Clan Chattan possessed a black wooden chanter (the finger-pipe of the bagpipes), which they acquired from an ethereal, ghostly bagpiper in 1396 during a clan battle. Legend has it that the chanter was dropped to the ground by the ghostly bagpiper, seized by the Clan Chattan piper, who played it, although wounded, till he died in the battle, which Clan Chattan won.

The chanter became the good luck symbol of Clan Chattan, and this good luck could be passed on by its loan to another clan. The McPherson Clan had temporary possession, and never lost a battle whilst in possession of the chanter. Strangely, the chanter did give good luck in battle to Prince Charles Edward Stuart – Bonnie Prince Charlie – while he was fighting alongside the McPherson Clan, but during the Battle of Culloden the Clan McPherson did not arrive in time to take part of the last battle on British soil.

Culloden Ghosts - The Last Battle on British Soil

Bonny Prince Charlie and his loyal Highlanders were defeated in battle on 16 April 1746, on Drummossie Moor, Culloden, by the Hanoverian Duke of Cumberland, who became known as the Butcher of Culloden for his barbaric treatment of wounded Highlanders, lying in the agony of dying on the battlefield. The German Hanoverian / English troops, aided by Lowland Scots Sassenach* troops, outnumbered the cold, weary, hungry Highlanders three to one, and acting on Cumberland's orders, gave no quarter during and after the battle.

The real reason for the No Quarter order was to secure the throne of Britain for the German Hanoverians by wiping out those Highlanders loyal to Prince Charles Edward Stuart – the *de jure* King Charles III – and making an example to other Highlanders not on the battlefield. In a few hours, the Highlanders lost the one-sided battle – 1,200 clansmen lay dead, and were buried where they died in communal graves. Their bones are still there. The Clan MacLachlan were in the forefront of the one-sided battle, and where they died it is said no heather will ever grow on their graves.

---

* A Sassenach is someone who is not a Highlander. The word is derived from Irish and Scots Gaelic 'Sasunnach', and originally meant Saxon English, but later came to mean Lowland Scot as opposed to Scots Highlanders as well.

Butcher Cumberland ordered guards placed around the wounded and dying Highlanders, with orders to shoot or bayonet any who tried to escape, or be given succour. Only one English officer had the honour to refuse to obey the Butcher's orders to kill defenceless Highlanders by offering his commission. The battlefield was rent with the agony of the mortally wounded dying a lonely, painful and terrible death. All who fell wounded were stripped of clothing and left to die in the cold, wet heather.

Squads of Hanoverian English and Scottish Lowlander Sassenachs on foot and horseback moved over the battlefield, seeking live Highlanders; if they found one, they bayoneted him to death in cold-blooded barbarity. One survivor, Alexander Macintosh of Essech, was badly wounded, and was found by redcoats. Feigning death, Macintosh was bayoneted in the back and buttocks, but the murdering redcoats moved off, leaving him to escape under the cover of darkness.

The ghosts of the dead Highlanders now haunt the always-silent battlefield of Culloden. A ghostly Highlander has been seen by the memorial cairn, and on the graves of those who died for their Prince and Scotland. Peter Underwood, the famous author of many books on ghosts and hauntings, informs the author of the following: on occasions, the dim form of a battle-weary Highlander has been seen in the vicinity of the Cairn, and one visitor, whilst looking at the Highlanders' graves, lifted a square of Stuart tartan which had blown down from the stone of the grave mound, and distinctly saw the body of a handsome, dark-haired

The field of Culloden.

Highlander, lying full-length on top of the grave mound. The visitor began to sense that the figure she was looking at was not of this world; his clothing was dirty, muddy, and old-fashioned, and his face had an unnatural pallor. She realised she was seeing a paranormal being, and turned away and fled from the Field.

When the wind blows over Culloden, some can still hear the cries of anguish. On some fine summer evenings, persons going over the moor can find themselves in the midst of the smoke and noise of a ghostly battle: steel on steel, roar of cannon, crackle of musket and pistol. Some say they saw the various clans involved in 1746, and identified their tartans. The Laird of Culdethel, a local gentleman riding a white horse, has been seen on occasion.

A pair of Prince Charles Edward Stuart tartan trews, said to be worn by him on the battlefield, is in the West Highland Museum. Several tartan weavers have reproduced the tartan, and although expensive – £250 per pair of trews – it is much in demand worldwide.

Prince Charles Edward Stuart haunts Culloden House, and there have been sightings of an army fighting in the sky. A troop of ghostly soldiers marches near the battlefield, led by an officer on a grey dragoon horse who wears a gold-laced hat and a blue Hussar pelisse or cloak. Some say he is the Butcher of Culloden, the German Cumberland himself, who always rode a grey horse.

The Cairn, Culloden.

When a present-day, mortal Highlander walks on the Field of Culloden, he can sense the pall of pain and death which still pervades the Field, which is unchanged since the awful battle. Granite stones mark the lines of the Clan Regiments. No British army regiment has 'Culloden' as a battle honour – the conduct of the Hanoverian English and Scottish Lowlander Sassenachs was a stain on the honour of the British Army. Cumberland, the Butcher of Culloden, as he became known, had issued the order 'No Quarter' before the battle, and it was carried out with fervour by most troops.

The original Culloden memorial cairn was a rude pile of stones erected in 1858, and then in 1881, the cairn as it is today was built by Duncan Forbes of Culloden, who also set up the headstones on the surrounding graves of the Clans. Hector Forbes of Culloden placed the cairn into the care of the National Trust of Scotland in 1944.

After the Battle of Culloden, the Micklegate Bar, York, was the scene of barbaric conduct, when twenty-two Jacobites were executed by beheading. Twenty of them were buried on Knavesmire, but the pro-Hanoverian government ordered that the heads of two, William Conolly and James Mayne, must be displayed on spikes mounted on poles set in iron sockets on Micklegate Bar. Again, the motive was to show to the townspeople of York the penalty for rising against the German Hanoverians.

Mickelgate, York, where twenty-two Jacobite heads were placed on spikes. (*Dayfield Graphics, York*)

The Jacobite heads remained on spikes until January 1754, when they were removed and taken away by an unknown person. The Mayor of York, a government supporter, proclaimed that a reward of £10 would be paid for the arrest of the persons responsible. When the powers that be in London heard of the theft of the heads they panicked, and the £10 reward was immediately increased to £112. In 1755, the culprit was found to be a local Roman Catholic named William Arundell, who had taken the heads for a Christian burial. Needless to say, he was arrested and charged with the alleged offence, and sentenced to two years in prison. The ghosts of the beheaded Jacobites sorrowfully haunt Micklegate Bar, where they were executed for supporting their Prince – Charles Edward Stuart. Headless ghosts have also been seen in the churchyard of Holy Trinity Church, Goodramgate, and York.

Castle Grant, Morayshire, Scotland, has the ghost of a piper who came from Culloden Battlefield to inform the Grants that the Clan had been defeated at Drumossie Moor, Culloden. He played his Great Highland Pipe twice round the castle then fell dead on the third round. There is a memorial cross on the castle wall, and the ghostly piper still plays his doleful lament.

Westbrook House, Godalming, Surrey, is reputed to be haunted by the ghost of Bonny Prince Charlie (Prince Charles Edward Stuart, The Young Pretender). Legend says that he met supporters there before the Rising of 1745, and dressed in a brown cloak to conceal his identity. In 1750, Prince Charles returned to London in disguise, and in a church in the Strand abjured the Roman Catholic religion and became a member of the Church of England. The Prince returned in disguise to England in the autumn of 1752, and again is believed to have stayed at the House, planning another attempt to seize the throne as Charles III. The Prince died in Rome on 31 January 1788, but his spirit is said to walk the gardens of Westbrook, where he had a sympathetic reception, still wearing a brown cloak. His ghost is also said to haunt the tragic Field of Culloden, and Culloden House, east of Inverness. The Prince's ghost has also been seen in the County Hotel, Dumfries, Dumfriesshire, where he slept in 1745.

The Prince's army marched over Souter Fell in Cumberland during the Rising of 1745, but local people, including Mr John Wren of Wilton Hall and his servant Daniel Stricket, saw it before, on Midsummer Eve, 23 June 1744, at about seven in the evening. They saw a ghostly army of soldiers, marching and riding horses, traverse the Fell near Mungrisdale. Again on Midsummer's Eve, 1745, the phantom army was seen by dozens of local people, soundlessly marching, with gun-carriages front and rear of the columns of soldiers.

Before the first Stuart Rebellion of 1715, an unprecedented electrical storm raged over the north of England, which was seen (correctly, as it turned out) as a bad omen for the Stuarts.

On the borders of Derbyshire and Staffordshire lies the village of Upper Mayfield, which has a road called Gallows Tree Lane, where, during Prince Charles' retreat from Derby in 1745, English soldiers executed Jacobite soldiers. Their ghosts still linger in the vicinity of the lane.

On 5 August 1748, at 2.00 p.m., a ghostly battle was seen in the sky, 5 miles west of Aberdeen, Scotland. One army was uniformed in blue and carried the Scottish Saltire flag of St Andrew, and the other army wore red and carried the Union Flag. The red army attacked the blue army twice, but was repulsed each time; the third time it attacked, it was defeated by the blue army and the spectral battle faded from sight.

A shop in Manchester has the ghost of a kilted, Jacobite Highlander – James Stuart – who marched to Manchester with Bonnie Prince Charlie, but was stabbed to death in the shop, which was once a house. Other Highlanders haunt Maghull, near Liverpool, at night, still trying to escape the fatal butchery of the approaching English troops. The sounds of mounted horsemen and the clash of steel on steel is heard; also, the sight of headless horsemen riding as night falls.

Simon Fraser, the Lord Lovat, was beheaded in London in April 1747 for his part in the Jacobite Uprising of 1746, and his ghost has been seen on a small island on Loch Morar, near Mallaig. The island was where he hid after the disaster at Culloden Field, but he was captured by Cumberland's Dragoons and taken to London. His ghost is described as 'a very heavy chap, with a fat florid face and suffering badly from gout'. (Courtesy of Peter Underwood)

The thirteenth-century Dunstaffnage Castle, Argyllshire, is haunted by the ghost of Flora MacDonald, who rescued Prince Charles Edward Stuart after the Battle of Culloden and took him to safety dressed as a maid named Betty Burke. Although a price of £30,000 had been placed on the Prince's head by the Hanoverians, not one Highlander betrayed him. In 1746, Flora was captured by the Hanoverians and imprisoned in the grim castle. She was later taken to the Tower of London, and became the toast of the society set after her release the following year. For some unknown reason her ghost haunts the grim castle, and has been seen several times.

The Ghostly Army in Glen Shira

In the summer of 1765, Glen Shira, Inverary, Argyllshire, was the scene of a vast, ghostly army marching six abreast. They wore red coats, carried flintlock muskets with fixed bayonets and Regimental Colours, and were led by an officer on a grey changer. The officer's uniform matched the uniform worn by the Duke of Cumberland (The Butcher of Culloden), who haunts the battlefield of Culloden. On each side of the ghostly redcoats straggled camp followers: women and children carrying pots and pans. (Report by Courtesy of Peter Underwood)

The Redcoat Sergeant's Ghost

After the Battle of Culloden, in an effort to crush the Highlanders' spirit, a declaration was made by Parliament that all tartans were forbidden to be worn, all weapons were to be handed in to the Hanoverian English army, and all Highlanders were to swear an oath not to challenge the Hanoverian English King again. Cumberland enforced this order without mercy, and sent out periodic patrols to carry it out it.

On one such foot and horse patrol in 1749, a Sergeant Arthur Davis, of Guise's 6th Regiment of Foot, who was in command of an eight-man platoon of soldiers in Glenshee (now the A93), Grampian Mountains, Perthshire, went hunting for game for their cooking pot. He did not return from his hunting trip. His soldiers carried on their patrol, and on arrival at Glenshee reported him missing. A search was carried out, but no body was found.

Local people began to report that they had seen a naked, ghostly man in Glenshee, who vanished when spoken to. Months later, it was reported that a ghostly sergeant dressed in a blue army coat had appeared to a local man in his bedroom and told him he was the missing Sergeant Davis. A short time later, the ghostly Sergeant Davis reappeared naked, and asked if his body could be given a proper burial from its present location in the undergrowth at the Hill of Christie nearby. On search of the hill, the rotting body of Sergeant Davis, in his blue army coat, was found, but with no money or valuables. He had been robbed and murdered. He was buried, and his ghost was seen no more.

Some years after Sergeant Davis had disappeared two local men – Duncan Terig and Alexander Mac Donald – were arrested and tried for his murder in Edinburgh. They were acquitted for lack of evidence. The ghost of Sergeant Arthur Davies has been seen at Dubhrach, Braemar, Aberdeenshire, perhaps unhappy at the not guilty verdict on his alleged murderers?

The Black Watch Ghost

The ghost of a one-time occupant, Duncan Campbell, whose cousin Donald Campbell was murdered by a Stewart of Appin, haunts Inverawe Castle, Argyll. The Stewart of Appin, knowing of Highland hospitality, boldly went to the Castle and asked for asylum to escape justice. He told Duncan Campbell that he had killed a man, but did not say who the man was. For several nights, the ghost of Donald appeared to his cousin Duncan and told him that the Stewart of Appin had killed him. Duncan could not break the Highland Code of Conduct, Honour and Hospitality, and refused to act against the Stewart of Appin. In desperation, the ghost of Donald said to Duncan, 'We will meet in Ticonderoga'.

On 17 July 1758, Duncan Campbell, by then a soldier in the Highland Black Watch regiment, was killed in action against the French at Fort Ticonderoga, and his body was interred at Fort Edward on the Hudson River. The ghostly prediction had proved correct, as the ghost of Duncan Campbell now haunts Inverawe castle. He had met his cousin Donald at Ticonderoga.

Headless Highlanders

Five headless highlanders haunt Dunphail Castle, near Forres in Grampian, northeast Scotland. The ghostly sounds of sword on sword steel, mixed with the sound of dying men breathing their last are also heard. The Cummings clan castle was under siege by the Earl of Moray, and five of the defenders, Alastair Cummings and his followers, fought their way out of the castle to re-supply their comrades with food. Returning with grain, they were captured by Moray's men and beheaded; then their heads were thrown to the castle defenders. Later, five headless skeletons were found, buried in a mound or barrow outside the castle.

The Ghostly Woman with No Hands

A bitter feud existed between the adjacent clans of Cummings of Rait Castle and the powerful Mackintoshes of Moy near Inverness. With slaughter in mind, the Cummings sent word to the Mackintoshes to come to a great dinner of venison and whisky. The suspicious Mackintoshes came with swords and pistols at the ready. The Ard Righ Cheil (Chief) of the Cummings found that his daughter had betrayed him, and without mercy cut off her hands. The maimed daughter – beside herself with pain –

threw herself off the battlements of Rait Castle to her death. The outraged advancing Mackintoshes gave bloody battle, and routed the Cummings and razed their castle. The sounds of ghostly battle sound in the ruined castle Rait, and a young woman with no hands and wearing a bloodstained dress haunts the desolate ruins.

The Cumberland Militia Ghost

In the eighteenth century, militias were raised on a county basis for home defence; they were also known as 'Trained Bands'. The Cumberland Militia was raised in 1760, and had as its Commanding Officer Sir James Lowther, First Earl of Lonsdale. The Militia had, on its red standard, the crest and cypher of Sir James in blue. The ancestral home of the Lowthers was Lowther Castle, Westmoreland, which Sir James Lowther inherited in 1784. Sir James was detested by the local populace and his mostly farmer tenants for his feudal manner. His nickname was 'Wicked Jimmy'.

He married by arrangement, but fell deeply in love with one of his tenant's daughters, but was unable to marry her as she was beneath his social station, so she became his mistress, and lived in style in a great manor house in the south of England. The mistress died suddenly, but Sir James refused to accept that she was dead, and kept her decomposing corpse lying in her bed. He then had her remains placed in a glass-topped coffin so that he could still see her at will. Eventually, she was buried in London and a company of his Cumberland Militia stood at her grave as mourners for three weeks.

Sir James returned north to Lowther Castle, but fell into a deep depression, which grew worse as time passed; he was still grieving for the love of his life. He continued to live at the castle, but began to let it decay and rot away, until he died alone in 1802. As his coffin was interred, it swayed as though someone alive was inside and trying to get out. The now near-derelict castle began to be haunted by strange noises, which emanated from the house, and the large stable complex where he had kept his coach and four in hand horses. Then local tenants began to report that, on moonlit nights, a ghostly coach and four had been seen rampaging through the neglected park and grounds of Lowther Castle – on the driver's box was the ghost of Sir James, raging and whipping his four in hand, and urging them to go faster and faster. Sir James' ghost is described as woebegone, dirty, smelly, and dressed in rags. He drives at breakneck speed around the castle then disappears into the stable block.

The Waterloo News Ghost

The 1815 Battle of Waterloo was won by the British (and other country's soldiers!) against the French. The victory news was sent back to Britain by horsemen and lighted victory beacons. At Caesar's Camp, Hampshire, and some 2 miles from Aldershot Army Barracks, the news was received by lighted beacon, and a soldier was ordered to run to Aldershot with the good news. En route to Aldershot, and running along what is known as Alma Lane, he was murdered by highwaymen. But his ghost is still making the journey with the good news, as the sound of heavy army boots is heard again and again, running in Alma Lane, Hampshire.

Shortly after Napoleon was routed at Waterloo, Belgian people saw ghostly soldiers from both sides fighting in the sky over the battlefield.

The Ghost of Napoleon

The British exiled Napoleon, Emperor of the French and Marshal of France, to the island of St Helena. His mother – Madame Bonaparte – lived in the Palazzo Bonaparte in Rome. On 5 May 1821, she was at home when a strange man appeared at her front door and requested of her servant that he must have an audience with her. The stranger wore a large cloak and a broad-brimmed hat pulled down over his face. He told the servant that he must speak at once with 'La Signora Madre'. Madam Bonaparte was informed, and said that she would see the stranger in her drawing room.

Entering the drawing room, the strange man covered his face, and said in a whisper, 'The Emperor is freed from his sufferings; today 5 May 1821, he died'. Turning abruptly, the stranger quickly left the room. Madame Bonaparte was stricken with grief – her son was dead! How did the stranger know? She asked the servants where the stranger had gone, but they replied that no one has passed through the house, other than the servants. Madame Bonaparte knew that news took weeks to travel from St Helena to Rome, but realised that the stranger was of familiar bearing and great presence and was somehow known to her.

Two and a half months later, Madame Bonaparte received the news that her son had indeed died on St Helena on 5 May 1821. The stranger was the ghost of her son Napoleon, who had appeared to her and her servant. It is said that the ghost of Napoleon periodically returns to the Palazzo Bonaparte in Rome, and appears at dusk in the drawing room.

Ghostly Soldiers of the American Civil and other Wars

During the American Civil War, which raged from 1861 to 1865 between the Northern Union and Southern Confederate armies, blue-jacketed and grey-trousered Union troops under Lieutenant General William Tecumseh Sherman swept through Tennessee, burning and laying waste the town of Gatlinburg in their path. The horror of Sherman's scorched earth policy remained in the folklore of Tennessee for many years.

On 14 July 1992, an American truck driver, thirty-eight-year-old Cletus Jasper, and his wife Bobby, were driving along US Route 441 towards the tourist town of Gatlinburg, Tennessee, at about 10.00 p.m., when they saw a long column of soldiers in dark blue uniforms marching alongside Route 441. The soldiers were carrying shoulder-slung rifles and carrying torches which gave off a greenish haze; however, Cletus Jasper and his wife could see right through the misty figures of the soldiers marching towards Gatlinburg. As Jasper approached the outskirts of the town, he saw the ghostly soldiers begin to fade from view in a mist, and finally disappear. A few hours later, the town of Gatlinburg erupted in a mysterious fire holocaust, which destroyed more than ten per cent of the business quarter. History had repeated itself.

Battle of Bloody Lane, Antietam, Maryland

On 17 September 1862, the bloodiest battle of the American Civil War took place at Antietam Creek, Sharpsburg, Maryland. Both sides took heavy casualties. The most horrific slaughter occurred in a sunken road, which owing to the slaughter, became known as 'Bloody Lane'; bodies were piled high when the Union troops enfiladed the Confederate troops and mowed them down. Casualties for both sides were assessed as somewhere around 5,445 dead.

Since the horrific battle, ghosts and ghostly sounds have been seen and heard on the battlefield: rifle fire, the clashing of steel on steel, and, amazingly, the Gaelic war cry of the 1,000-strong Irish Brigade '*Faugh a Balaugh*' ('Clear the Way'), who lost half their strength in battle (540 men).

Many of the dead who fell at Burnside Bridge haunt their place of death, still playing their drums into battle, and the light and flames of campfires are seen. Where the Confederate Headquarters and Field Hospital were located on the battlefield, a phantom figure appears, and voices are heard. At St Paul's church in Sharpsburg, which was used as a hospital, the dying screams of many men are heard, dying in agony and calling for their loved ones.

The Arsenal at Harper's Ferry, (then Virginia), USA

Before the American Civil War, Harper's Ferry was an important arms-producing arsenal (the surviving firearms are highly prized, and fetch large prices). On 16 October 1859, the slavery abolitionist, the wild-eyed John Brown (of *John Brown's Body* ballad fame) attacked and seized the arsenal with a small force of fifteen men, and took it by storm. Four of the attacking party were black men.

Brown's party opened fire on the local people, killing a black man. The locals replied with rifle fire, killing one of Brown's men, also a black man, who was mutilated by the locals and fed to hogs in a nearby alley.

Militia were sent to Harpers Ferry, and in a fierce firefight most of Brown's men were killed. Brown was captured and hanged for treason at Charlestown on 2 December 1859. According to legend, when he was on the scaffold, Brown's wild eyes began to shine brightly with a weird light, even after he was hanged. Wax was poured over the ghastly eyes to cover the unearthly glow. Brown's ghost haunts the scene of his hanging, and round the door of the Arsenal; a black dog is at his heels. Some say that he poses for tourists' photographs! The Negro, shot by the locals and left in an alley for hogs to feed on, is reported to walk what is now named Hog Alley. He still wears the hat and trousers he was killed in.

The sounds of men marching to a drum beat are heard along Ridge Street on occasion. Ghostly, uniformed Civil War troops infest South Mountain, near Harper's Ferry, still lighting campfires and cooking their meals. St Peter's church has the ghost of a mortally wounded soldier, who was taken into the church for medical aid, but to no avail. Other phantom smells and sounds abound: the smell of sulphur from the barrels of firing cannon, and the deadly clash of bayonet on bayonet.

Gettysburg Battle Hauntings

The Battle of Gettysburg, Pennsylvania raged from 1 to 3 July 1863, with some 165,000 soldiers involved, of which there were some 50,000 casualties.

The worst day of death was the third day, when 12,000 Confederate soldiers attacked Union positions across open ground, and were decimated by artillery fire. Only some 2-300 reached Union Lines. When the battle ended, dead soldiers littered the battlefield – most were never buried and left where they fell.

The ghosts of the slaughtered soldiers haunt the area of the battlefield and the countryside around. A regiment of ghostly soldiers has been seen carrying out drill under the hill named Little Round Top. To those who witnessed the event it seemed real, but they were told by locals that it was ghostly.

Confederate Brigadier-General William Barksdale was badly wounded, and taken to Hummelbaugh House to be treated. He died outside the front door, crying for water. His spirit still haunts the front of the house, still crying for water.

Rose Farm buildings were a field hospital, and many soldiers died there in agony. Most of the dead were buried round the farm, but their remains were exhumed in 1963 and reburied elsewhere. But still, ghostly soldiers on horseback continue their long-dead battle, and the remaining gravestones are sometimes lit with glowing lights.

Pennsylvania Hall, Gettysburg College, was also used for a major hospital, and the occupants have seen Civil War doctors operating on wounded men, removing arms and legs. A ghastly sight.

The Cashtown Inn – some short distance from the battlefield – has a Confederate soldier ghost who frequents the upper floor.

The horrific battle of Shiloh resulted in 20,000 dead, and it was reported that the river nearby ran red with their blood. Again and again, the sounds of battle – cannon and rifle fire, and the clash of steel on steel – are heard over the battlefield.

The Battle of Chickamauga was fought in Tennessee in 1863, on 19 and 20 September. There were 35,000 casualties – most of them dead – and at first it was a victory for the South, but a few weeks later, at Chattanooga, the North finally won. The mass of dead soldiers was buried where they fell, some in large mass graves with no headstones or personal markers. All over the battlefield at night, ghosts can be seen wandering, as though lost. Flickering lights are seen at night, reputed to be the ghosts of women searching for their loved ones in the carnage of the dead. A headless cavalry officer has been seen at full gallop.

The most famous soldier ghost is an apparition called 'Ole Green Eyes'. He is the ghost of a Confederate solder who had his head blown off by cannon fire. His head was buried, but his body was blown to pieces by the volleys of cannon fire which raked the Southern lines. He wanders over the battlefield looking for his missing body, with his green eyes glowing and his terrible sounds of moaning.

Ghosts of the Battle of Cedar Creek, Virginia

The Battle of Cedar Creek, Virginia, was fought in October 1864, between Union and Confederate forces, with the Union side winning after a short,

sharp, bloody encounter. Battlefield visitors with no knowledge of the events say that they have heard the sounds of the battle, the screams of the dead and dying, the calls of bugles and the roaring of cannon. The local church, which was used as a hospital for wounded during the battle, is said to echo with the sounds of wounded soldiers. The battlefield has been called 'one of the most haunted battlefields of the Shenandoah'.
(Courtesy of Peter Underwood)

Ghosts of the Battle of San Pasqual, California

The battle of San Pasqual, San Diego County, California, took place on 6 December 1847, between Mexican and American troops, during the Mexican-American War. The Americans used dragoons, who were soldiers on horseback, but would fight on foot if required by circumstance. Opposing them were the flamboyant Mexican lancers, who were cavalry only and used as shock troops. At the end of the battle, the dead of both sides were buried on the battlefield in mass graves, over which hang an aura of cold blasts of icy air. On the anniversary of the battle, ghostly Mexican lancers and American dragoons have been seen on the battlefield, still in combat, and the scream of dead and dying soldiers are heard with blasts of icy air round parts of the battlefield.

Ghostly Armies in Germany, Croatia, and Crete

Just after the Franco Prussian War of 1870, which the French lost, anti-French feeling was running high in Germany. In 1872, in the town of Boully, Germany, local people saw the redoubtable French Zouave troops waving their regimental colours in the glass of the windowpanes of their houses. Prussian troops were called, and smashed the glass panes in which the French troops could still be seen until the glass was broken into minute fragments, and the French soldiers could no longer be seen.

A ghostly troop of men and horses are alleged to lay waste any buildings along the route between the castles of Rodenstein and Schnellert, Germany. The last official recorded visit of the wild horde was in June 1764, when they laid waste houses that stood in their path.

When General von Cosel died in 1785, at Ujest, Silesia, his military cortege was accompanied by a ghostly escort of soldiers marching in the sky above, and along his funeral route.

One of the bloodiest battles of the Greek War of Independence was fought on the island of Crete, at Frangocastella. A Turkish army of 900

men attacked 385 Greek soldiers on 17 May 1828, and slaughtered them to the last man. Over the ensuing years, there have been reports of the two ghostly Greek and Turkish armies re-appearing at dawn on 17 May and re-fighting the battle. At Varasidin, Croatia, on 1, 2 and 3 August, 1888, an aerial army, led by a warrior with a flaming sword, was seen by hundreds marching across the sky then disappearing without trace.
(Courtesy of Peter Underwood)

The Phantom Black Dog

Ballechin House, Aberfeldy, Scotland, was the estate of the Steuarts. In 1873, a Major Robert Steuart was in residence, and had often said he would return after death in the form of a black dog. It is a Scots saying that someone 'has a black dog on their back' when they are sulking and bad-tempered! When the Major died, the dogs on the estate were put to sleep by a relative who had inherited the property.

Immediately, the estate began to be haunted by a prowling black dog that tried to enter the closed main door by hurling itself against the sturdy wood. Dragging footsteps were heard in the corridors; screams and heart-rending cries were heard from empty rooms.

French Foreign Legion Ghosts

In May 1912, three companies of Legionnaires were making their way to an isolated desert fort in Algeria, when local tribesmen ambushed them and, in the ensuing fire-fight, killed five Legionnaires. The Arabs ran off, and the Legionnaires immediately buried their five comrades in the sand, with heavy stones over the graves to prevent jackals digging up the bodies. Some two weeks after the firefight, a Legionnaire Rene Dupre was on night guard, when he saw a solitary figure in the moonlight staggering towards the fort. Unslinging his rifle, Dupre prepared to challenge the figure when he realised he could see through the figure, whom he now saw was wearing Legion uniform. Dupre called out the Guard, and pointed out the ghostly figure to them. One of the Guard recognised the figure as a Legionnaire Leduc, one of the five killed in the firefight. As the Guard watched, they saw the ghostly figure staggering about in a zig-zag manner then vanish from sight.

The ghost of Leduc was seen again four nights later, still staggering and walking in a zigzag manner, before disappearing. A few nights later, Dupre was again on night guard when he saw another figure, walking about in a zigzag manner as though looking for something on the ground. Dupre identified the figure as French Legion Chef (Sergeant) Schmidt, who had also been killed in the recent ambush. The odd behaviour of the two ghostly Legionnaires mystified those who saw them, until someone suggested it could be that they were looking for each other, even though they were now ghosts.

Two weeks later, the entire garrison of the fort saw two figures marching off towards the skyline. They were the ghosts of Leduc and Schmidt! As the two ghostly Legionnaires reached the skyline, one raised his arm in farewell and the two disappeared, reunited in death. They were never seen again.

First World War Ghosts

As a symbolic grave for the soldiers who died in France during the First World War and have no known grave, the body of an unknown soldier from the battlefield of Flanders was buried in Westminster Abbey, London. It is said that the ghostly figure of a muddy, wounded soldier appears in the Abbey on rare occasions.

In the abbey at Bath, Avon, is a monument to the local regiment, the Somerset Light Infantry. Nearby is a stone pillar, where in 1926, some eight years after the Great War, the likeness of a soldier in full marching order with .303 rifle on his shoulder was seen in the stone of the pillar.

Belfield House, Perth, Scotland, was occupied during the First World War by the 1st and 2nd Battalions of the Highland Artillery Brigade. In 1915, the house was plagued with hauntings, which had an adverse effect on the morale of the troops billeted there.

Longleat House, Wiltshire, stately home of the Thynne family since the Reformation, has a ghost in the library. He is Sir John Thynne, who was killed in action in France in 1916, leading his soldiers from the front. He has been seen sitting in the Red Library reading books, and has been mistaken for one of the thousands of visitors who flock to Longleat.

The Coliseum Theatre in St Martin's Lane in London is reputed to be haunted by the uniformed ghost of a First World War soldier. He walks down the dress circle gangway and turns into the second row, just before the house lights are lowered for the on-stage performance. The ghost has been recognised as a soldier who spent his last night at the theatre before leaving for the battlefields of France. He was first seen on 3 October 1918 – this was the date he was killed in action. (Courtesy of Peter Underwood)

During late August 1914, reports began to appear in British newspapers that during the hard-fought withdrawal of the British Army from Mons,

Belgium, on 26 August 1914, spectral soldiers – knights in armour, bowmen and glowing angels – had appeared, and fought on the British side against the advancing Germans. A cavalry colonel from Bristol swore that his retreating cavalry column was accompanied on both flanks by ghostly cavalry who protected them from the Germans during a vital twenty-minute period. Many German, French and British soldiers stated that they had seen the ghostly armies fighting on the British side. German soldiers' morale sank – they wore leather belts with the buckle embossed *Gott Mit Uns* (God is With Us), and yet they thought the British were aided by some unearthly army. On the British side, morale was at its peak – some unearthly spirit was fighting alongside them – so they were able to hold their line, although 15,000 French and British soldiers were killed in battle. Perhaps these dead soldiers' spirits returned to the battlefield on the side of their comrades. The site of the fifteenth-century Battle of Agincourt is near Mons, and perhaps the ghosts of archers and soldiers from the ancient battle returned to fight on the side of the hard-pressed British and French soldiers.

A Mr Arthur Machen had a short story entitled 'The Bowmen' published in the *London Evening News* on 29 September 1914, in which he told of St George – the patron saint of England – appearing on the battlefield with

The War Memorial, Mons.

ghostly archers from the 1415 Battle of Agincourt, and placing themselves between the opposing German and British armies. Machen later said he had made the story up, but a Harold Begbie also wrote a book, *On the Side of the Angels*, in 1915 which listed many accounts of the ghostly soldiers who fought with the British; these statements were given to Begbie by soldier witnesses who had fought at Mons, before Machen wrote his short story.

A Ghostly Billiards Player

The owner of a large property volunteered for the army in 1915 as an officer, but was discharged due to a concealed illness which was discovered. He returned home to his property in the English Midlands in 1916, but brooded on his being discharged as unfit for service so much that he shot himself in his billiards room at Christmas 1916.

During the Second World War, the property was requisitioned as an Army officers' mess; in 1943, an army lieutenant colonel entered the billiards room and found an officer, dressed in an obsolete First World War Kitchener's Army blue uniform, already there playing billiards. The colonel asked for a game, and played against the other officer until the dinner gong sounded, whereupon the game ceased, and the strangely uniformed officer walked out of the billiards room. At dinner, the colonel asked who the strangely uniformed officer was - no one knew, except a mess waiter who had been in service in the house for many years; it was the ghost of the First World War officer, who was known as Master Willie, who had shot himself whilst in the billiards room, during a fit of depression at being rejected by the Army. Three nights later, two young army officers saw the blue-uniformed ghost by the billiard table.

The Grenadier Card-Playing Ghost

Knightsbridge, London, is the home of the Grenadier Guards, and the local pub is named The Grenadier. Legend has it that Guards officers were playing cards in the pub, when one was caught cheating. His outraged colleagues meted out flogging as a summary punishment, to such an extent that he later died in the cellar of the pub. His reputed ghost has been seen coming up the stairs from the cellar, and in a bedroom, each autumn.

The Cavalry Ghost in the Cellar

In 1900, the old Mansion House in York, by the side of the River Ouse, was haunted by the sound of slow, heavy footsteps, and of metal ringing and jangling on the floors and stairs. From the cellar came the sound of something being thrown down heavily on the flagstones. Some three or four years later, workmen were repairing the flagstones in the cellar when they came upon a human skeleton. It was examined by police and a pathologist, and found to be of a large, heavily-built man. By his feet were two rusty cavalry spurs, one with a broken rowel, which was the cause of the jangling sound made by his ghost: as he moved, the broken rowel struck the ground. Enquiries as to his identity were negative.

The Cheese Room Soldier Ghost

At the seventeenth-century Higher Filford Farm, Bowood, near Bridport, Dorset, the ghost of an old, bearded soldier frequently haunts the room where cheese used to be stored to mature. He is dressed in a grey coat with silver buttons, and epaulettes on the shoulders, a tricorne hat turned up at both sides, and uses a forked-handled stick as a walking stick. He disappears backwards through the wall when challenged.

Lawrence of Arabia's Ghost

The famous Lawrence of Arabia (Thomas Edward Lawrence) enlisted in the Royal Air Force in August 1922 under the name of John Hume Ross. He was discharged in January 1923, and a month later, in February, enlisted in the Royal Tank Corps under the assumed name of Thomas Edward Shaw. He bought a small cottage at Cloud's Hill, Bovington, Dorset, in 1925. It took him ten years to restore the cottage to its former glory. There he entertained many famous writers, and worked on his magnificent book *Seven Pillars of Wisdom*. Lawrence reenlisted in the Royal Air Force in August 1925.

In August 1925, whilst serving at RAF College Cranwell, Lawrence bought a powerful George Brough Superior motorcycle, registered number RK 4907, which he christened 'Boanerges', and on which he loved to ride at speed. This was one of several Brough motorcycles owned by Lawrence.

In 1935 he retired from the Royal Air Force, and took up full residence at Cloud's Hill, and continued to ride motorcycles at speed about the Dorset countryside. At about 11.20 a.m. on 13 May 1935, Lawrence suffered a fatal traffic accident whilst riding a motorcycle at speed on the road from

Lawrence's cottage at Cloud's Hill, Dorset.

Lawrence's grave at Moreton, Dorset, complete with mysterious red rose. (*Dorset County Council, Lara Nixey and Mark Simons*)

Bovington camp to Clouds Hill. He swerved to avoid colliding with two boys on bicycles, and crashed. Lawrence was taken to Bovington Army Camp Hospital in a coma, and died on 21 May 1935.

At the Inquest held later, an army corporal, Ernest Catchpole, stated that he had seen Lawrence on his motor cycle, travelling at about 50 to 60 miles per hour when abreast of Clouds Hill Camping Ground, and coming from the direction of Bovington Army Camp. He also stated that he had seen Lawrence on his motorcycle pass a black car, which was travelling in the opposite direction quite safely. He then said that Lawrence had swerved to avoid two boys on bicycles travelling in the same direction. When Dorset Police questioned the two boys, they denied any knowledge of a mysterious black car.

Lawrence's funeral was held in the church at Moreton, not far from Clouds Hill, on 21 May 1935. He was laid to rest in the churchyard, and his grave is a Mecca for his legion of admirers. A single red rose is often left on his grave – it is not known by whom.

A ghostly figure in the flowing white Arabic dress which Lawrence wore in the desert has been reported in the area, and entering his cottage. The roar of the powerful ghostly Brough Superior motorcycle ridden by Lawrence still sounds on local Dorset roads, usually just before dawn. Expert witnesses have stated that the sound of the Brough Superior is unmistakeable.

Lawrence in Arab dress, *c.* 1917.

His Cloud's Hill cottage is now maintained by the National Trust, and is open for viewing, and well worth a visit. The author has visited it, and was impressed with the peaceful, learned atmosphere. Downstairs, the tiny cottage has a minute kitchen, and the adjacent bedroom wall is lined with books, his Royal Air Force-issue bed space rug is by his bed. Upstairs, there is but one large music room, which was used by Lawrence to entertain his famous guests. His wind-up gramophone with a large trumpet still dominates the room, and his presence can be felt by some of the frequent visitors who are aware of his presence.

Cloud's Hill is just off the A352, and is on the secondary road sign-posted as The Tank Museum and Bovington Army camp. The Wareham Museum, East Street, Wareham, has a collection of Lawrence memorabilia, and the Curator, Mike O' Hara, will make anyone welcome. He is a mine of information on Lawrence of Arabia, and is an author. Also, there is an effigy of Lawrence in St Martin's Church, Wareham. All of which is a must for his admirers.

The American Soldier Ghost on his Motorcycle

The town of Elmore, Ohio, USA, has the legend of a ghostly, headless young soldier on a motorcycle, which roars through the town each year on the anniversary of his sudden death on a motorcycle.

The soldier returned from the First World War in 1918, and bought a powerful motorcycle to impress his girlfriend. Riding the machine at speed to his girlfriend's house, he was devastated to learn that she preferred another man. In a fit of temper and shock he roared off on the motorcycle at speed, but lost control on a sharp bend, and went over into a ravine and was decapitated. His ghost appears on 21 March each year, still riding his motor cycle at speed, then vanishing abruptly at the spot where he died.

The Ghostly Castle - Burned by the IRA

During the Irish Civil War, the Earl of Bandon and his family occupied Castle Bernard in County Cork, Ireland. On 21 June 1921, during a guest and family dinner party, the local IRA entered the castle, and forced all to leave at gunpoint and stand outside. The IRA then put the castle to the torch, and the castle and its contents were destroyed by fire and became a ruin. The IRA took prisoner Earl Bandon, and police began a search, which caused the IRA to move their prisoner from safe house to safe house during the hours of darkness. Three weeks later, the Earl was released in a poor state. Locals say that the infamous burning of the castle has been seen as a ghostly re-enactment, on the anniversary of the night it was burned down by the IRA. The castle is still in ruins.

The Ghost of Wilton Castle - Burned by the IRA

The local IRA burnt down Wilton Castle, Wexford, Ireland, in 1923, after it had been occupied by the same family since 1695. Nearby was the village of Ballinapeirce, where lived a Captain Archibald Jacob, of the local Yeoman Rangers. He was also a local magistrate, and was a harsh judge of those brought before him; he was reputed to use torture to gain confessions from accused. He was hated for the tyrannical abuse of his powers as a magistrate. On 29 December 1836, the hated Captain Jacob was returning from a County Ball at Wilton Castle when he was killed by a fall from his hunter horse at a spot called the Black Stream, a short distance from Wilton Castle. He was killed instantly, and his death, it was said, was no loss to the local people. Shortly after his death, the ghost of Yeoman Ranger Captain Jacob began to appear at Wilton Castle and the Black Stream. A service of exorcism was held in the castle by a Catholic priest, and at the end of the ceremony the ghost of the tyrannical captain appeared, then abruptly disappeared – never to be seen again.

The Crimean War Hospital Nurse

The old Victoria Military Hospital, Netley, Southampton, was built between 1855 and 56, and over the years housed thousands of soldier patients from the various wars since. One legend is that a nurse, who served during the Crimean War, committed suicide at the Hospital and has been seen as a ghost. The hospital was demolished in 1966. There is, or was, the ghost of a nurse dressed in obsolete uniform, which was always seen in a certain corridor, and is thought to be that of Florence Nightingale, who had the Hospital built and worked there and campaigned vigorously to keep the Hospital open – she did not want the building demolished.

The Cambridge Military Hospital Ghostly Sister

The 100-year-old Cambridge Military Hospital has the legend of a Nursing Sister of the Queen Alexandra Imperial Nursing Service haunting Ward

13. It stems from a Nursing Sister who inadvertently administered a fatal dose of medication to a patient and afterwards, in her remorse, committed suicide by throwing herself over the hospital balcony to her death. She has been seen on many occasions by patients, and, in 1969, by a night duty Orderly Sergeant. She has a reputation of being a kindly, benign spirit who mainly appears when the nursing staff is under pressure.

The British Military Sentry at an American Base

During 1944, hundreds of American soldiers were shipped to England in preparation for D-Day, 6 June 1944. Accommodation was scarce, and troops were billeted where there was space for tents and rooms in barracks. An old First World War army barracks had been demolished before the Second World War broke out, and on the site were built ablutions (service name for lavatories). The ablutions were built right over what had been the old barracks main gate, which had been guarded by armed sentries who had marched up and down in front of the gate.

Just before D-Day, when the American troops were embarking for France, reports began to surface of a First World War British Army soldier, dressed in a 1914 uniform and carrying a .303-inch Lee Enfield rifle, haunting the ablutions. Americans were frightened out of their wits by his presence; one American said that he had been in the ablutions when the ghostly British soldier was marching up and down, as if on sentry duty. Being friendly, the American spoke to the British soldier, but was ignored! Then the sentry ghost turned, and walked through the American soldier!

Enquiries were made of the resident British liaison officers, who knew of the ghost and his sentry-duty marching in the ablutions. In 1918, a British soldier on guard duty at the now-demolished barracks gate had been murdered there, but his ghost still kept marching, still obeying his last orders!

The Witch of Scrapfaggot Green

Local legend has it that a stone boulder at Great Leigh, Essex, holds down the spirit of the Witch of Scrapfaggot Green. In October 1944, a US Army bulldozer was used to move the boulder, whereupon strange disturbances began to happen in the village. The church clock refused to work for no apparent reason, the church bells rang with no bell ringers in the church, gates were opened mysteriously, and objects flew through the air in classic poltergeist activity. The famous ghost hunter Harry Price was invited to

The St Anne's Castle, Great Leigh, Essex, the oldest inn in England, dating from 1171. (*Elli Constantatue, Essex County Council*)

affect a cure, and suggested that the moved boulder be replaced. On 11 October 1944, the Witch's boulder was replaced, and the manifestations ceased.

Field Marshal Rommel

The famous – and respected by British Forces – commander of the Second World War German *Afrika Korps*, Field Marshal Erwin Johannes Eugen Rommel, possessed some kind of foreknowledge of what was about to happen. His *Afrika Korps* called it *Fingerspitzengefuhl* – on 25 November 1942, he was standing with his staff officers on a bare North African desert, when he suddenly told them 'We must move from here'. Rommel and his officers moved a few hundred yards away, and within minutes British shells were landing on where the Germans had been standing. In July 1944, Rommel was wounded in an RAF fighter air attack on his staff car in Normandy, and retired to recuperate at his home near Stuttgart. There he began to have some foreknowledge of the destiny awaiting him. On 13 October 1944, Hitler gave Rommel a stark choice – suicide, or dishonour in a Peoples' Court, where he would stand trial accused of being involved in the bomb plot to blow up Hitler.

Field Marshal Rommel dressed in *Afrika Korps* uniform.

Field Marshall Rommel committed suicide by cyanide poisoning. Rommel was given a hypocritical State Funeral, and a State pension was paid to his wife Lucie Maria and his son Manfred, who after the war ended became *Oberburgmeister* (Mayor) of Stuttgart. In 1999, I spoke on the telephone to Herr Manfred Rommel regarding his famous father, and found him most interesting and polite.

'Herman the German'

Bovington Camp, Dorset, has a famous Tank Museum, where tanks of various nations are displayed. One exhibit is a captured Second World War German Panzer Tiger tank which has been restored to its wartime condition, and on several occasions custodians (one of whom is an ex-long service policeman) of the Museum reported seeing the figure of a German officer peering in through the windows at the Tiger tank. However, the lower sills of the windows are 8 feet from the ground, so the ghostly German – nicknamed 'Herman the German' by the staff – must be very tall, or is floating in the air!

German Tiger tank, Bovington Tank Museum. (*Tank Museum, Wareham, Mrs Janis Tait, Librarian*)

The Dieppe Raid

On Wednesday 19 August 1942, a joint British and Canadian assault force of some 6,100 men with thirty tanks landed at Dieppe, in German occupied France, in what was a rehearsal for the D-Day invasion of Europe (6 June, 1944). The attack was a bloody, tragic failure, and the Allies suffered heavy casualties. The losses were 4,340 men, including 1,179 dead and 2,190 PoWs, thirty tanks, HMS *Berkeley* (a destroyer), and 100 aircraft.

Nine years later, on 4 August 1951, two British women were on holiday at Puys, Dieppe, one of the invasion beaches for the Dieppe Raid. At 4.20 a.m. on Saturday 4 August, they both awoke to the sounds of battle, guns firing, shells landing, men screaming, aircraft locked in aerial combat, which continued until they died away at 7.00 a.m. Feeling sure everyone else in the hotel must have heard the noise of battle, the two sisters made enquiries, but *they* were the only persons who had heard the ghostly re-enactment of the Dieppe Raid.

Ghostly Clouds

On Sunday 8 November 1942, three Allied military task forces began landing men and equipment in Operation Torch, the invasion of North Africa. The immense force of 673,000 troops in their invasion ships and barges lay exposed on the open sea to the might of the German Luftwaffe in the clear skies over the fleet. Inexplicably, a dark protective cloud formed over the exposed fleets, shielding them from the German attacks. This protective cloud formation remained over the fleets for the next ten days, enabling the troops to get ashore.

During the Korean War in the 1950s, United States Air Force B17 bombers were on a bombing mission over Korea when the aircrews saw, in the white cumulus clouds around them, what appeared to be the giant figure of Christ, with his right arm raised in Benediction among the cloud formations.

Modern Sightings of Scottish Ghosts

During November 1956, two young men were on a camping holiday on the Cuillin Hills, Isle of Skye, Scotland, when they were rudely awakened at 3.00 a.m. by the sound of someone running over the ground outside their tent. Looking out, they saw a band of kilted Highlanders armed to the teeth, running over the ground. At about 4.00 the next morning, they were again asleep in their tent when they heard noises from outside their tent. Looking out, they saw what appeared to be the same band of kilted Highlanders, tattered, battle-stained and despondent, despairingly lurch across their field of view and disappear. On making enquiries of the locals, they were told many others had witnessed the ghostly Highlanders who were retreating from action, probably against the English after the Battle of Culloden in 1746, or from some inter-clan battle. As the Highlanders were wearing kilts, it would appear that they were not from earliest times, as the *feile beag* kilt (little kilt) as such did not appear in Scotland until *c.* 1600.

In November 1960, many people alleged that they saw ghostly armies fighting on the site of the Battle of Otterburn (19 August 1388 – Northumberland). The battle was between the Scots of the Douglas Clan, and the English under the Percys, led by Henry Percy, known as Harry Hotspur, and the battle went to the Scots.

It was said that local people had seen the phantom soldiers, both knights in armour and men at arms, on several occasions; usually the ghostly protagonists appear on the A68 road, which now runs through what was the then battlefield then vanish as the villagers watch. The night before the no-quarter battle, the Chief of the Clan Douglas dreamed that he saw 'a dead man win a fight'. The next day, the Chief of the Douglas Clan died fighting on the Field of Otterburn! He was the dead man; his clansmen had concealed his dead body in a clump of bracken from the enemy, and fought valiantly to overcome the English soldiers and force them to surrender.

Father John's Ghost

Brede Place, by Rye, Sussex, was originally built about 1350 by monks and knights. Legend has it that one monk – Father John – haunts the house. During the Second World War, the Army took over the house as accommodation for troops – mostly officers. Some Canadian officers complained that ghostly monks, who hid their clothing and caused tables and chairs to move of their own accord, were harassing them. Consternation was caused one day, when the ghost of Father John was seen to walk through a group of soldiers in a passageway. Also haunting Brede Place there is the severed-body ghost of Sir Goddard Oxenbridge, a knight who was sawn in half on Groaning Bridge in 1537 for the alleged offence of eating children. The ghostly, severed knight walks between the Bridge and Brede Place.

The Sergeants' Mess Ghost

The Friary at Bergholt, Essex, was originally St Mary's Abbey for Benedictine nuns. During the Second World War, it was requisitioned for army use. One room in the Friary was adopted as a Sergeants' Mess, and was much frequented by them. However, it was found that an old door which led into the Mess would open of its own accord at 10.50 p.m. each night; at the same time the air temperature would drop in the classic warning of a ghostly presence. Nothing was seen, and although observation was kept on both sides of the door at once, nothing was detected, and the door still opened of its own accord. A young soldier was asleep one night, when he was awakened by the sound of his bedroom door opening. As he sleepily watched, he saw a misty form appear, and he felt two ice-cold hands feeling his face. He screamed in terror, and the shape disappeared abruptly.

The author had a similar experience at RAF Netheravon, but he told the ghost to go away – and the ghost vanished! (Courtesy of Peter Underwood)

Bergholt Friary, Essex. (*Chris Underwood, courtesy Peter Underwood*)

The Ghostly Sikh Soldier

During the Second World War, January 1942 saw the Japanese army sweep into what was then Burma, and engage in combat with the British 14th Army, composed of British and Indian troops, who put up a fierce resistance, but by 20 May 1942, all Burma was under Japanese occupation. Part of 14th Army was the Royal Corps of Signals Regiment, whose radio communications were vital to operations.

During a Japanese field artillery bombardment, an off-duty Royal Signals corporal took cover near a Burmese pagoda. Thinking this was good safe cover, the corporal – as was normal off-duty army practice – decided to catch up on his sleep, in spite of the continuing Japanese artillery barrage.

A few minutes into sleep, the corporal was woken by a voice. Sitting up, he saw an Indian Sikh soldier before him. The Sikh soldier told him to report to his commanding office at Royal Signal Headquarters at once. The corporal was mystified, as there were no Indian Sikh solders within many miles. Reporting to his officer at Signals Headquarters, the corporal was told that no one had sent for him as he was not needed, and they did not even know his off-duty location.

Returning to what had been his safe cover at the pagoda he was appalled at what he saw. Japanese artillery shells had blown the top off one of the spires, and masonry had fallen onto the very spot where he had been sleeping.

The ghostly Sikh soldier had saved his life, by making him report to his headquarters before the masonry fell on the spot where he had been sleeping. No explanation was ever forthcoming from any quarter.

Adolf Hitler's Ghostly Voice

It has been reported in Germany that Adolf Hitler's distinctive, high-pitched ranting voice has been heard on Hamburg radio, and on tape in Stockholm, shouting 'We live, we live, we are not dead'. No one could identify the origin of the Hamburg voice, which was accompanied by the sound of wailing Second World War air raid warning sirens, and the roar of aircraft engines overhead. The voice has been identified as Hitler's by checking against the mass of recordings made by the dictator. But the words, 'we are not dead', etc. are not in any recording. (Report by Wehrmacht Soldier Hans Kutcher)

The Legless Gurkha Solider Ghost

Some years after the Second World War, the Police Training Centre staff and some 2,000 police recruits at Ipoh, Malaya, were horrified and in terror of the ghost of a legless Gurkha soldier, who had been shot and killed by terrorists in the jungle.

The Police Centre staff found that the recruits were afraid to go on patrol in the jungle until the remains of the dead soldier were exhumed and cremated, then returned to his family in far-away Nepal.

Still in Malaysia, the uniformed ghost of a Second World War Japanese officer, carrying a pistol and wearing, in a scabbard, a Samurai Katana sword, walks up Kuala Selangor Hill, to the house which he occupied during the occupation of Malaysia by the Japanese during the Second World War. When he enters the house he disappears from sight.

The Colonel's Ghostly Motor Car

On the high-speed main-line level crossing near Conington, 6 miles south of Peterborough, Cambridgeshire, stands a level crossing which is now automatic, but before 1970 was manually operated.

During the Second World War, German army prisoners of war (PoWs) were employed on farms in the Conington Fen area, and were transported to and from work by lorry. Of necessity, the lorry had to be driven over the level crossing. On a foggy morning in the mid-1940s, six of the German PoWs were killed when a railway engine struck the lorry they were in, when visibility was limited on the unmanned crossing.

On 16 October 1948, at about 5.30 p.m., a Colonel A. H. Mellows drove his black vintage car up to the still-unmanned level crossing, and stopped to allow his passenger, a Mr A. Percival, to get out and open the level crossing gates. For some unknown reason, Colonel Mellows moved his car forward, directly into the path of an express train travelling at high speed. He was killed instantly. Mr Percival was uninjured.

With seven deaths on the level crossing during the 1940s, reports began to circulate locally that the ghosts of those who had met a violent death on it haunted the crossing. An old, 1940s-vintage black car has been seen approaching the crossing, but always disappeared before the signalman could open the gates. Is the colonel still trying to cross the level crossing where he met his death in 1948?

The Windsor Park Ghostly Sentry and Others

Windsor Great Park has the uniformed ghost of a sentry who committed suicide by shooting himself in the 1920s, when on patrol duty in the Long Walk; he stills patrols the Park, and has been seen repeatedly. In life, the sentry had been of a sullen, morose disposition, but when seen as a ghost he was happy and smiling.

In 1864, a sentry at the Tower of London was court-martialled for fainting on sentry duty. At his court martial he stuck to his story: that he had seen a large apparition in front of him when on his patrol walk. He challenged the figure, then, when he did not get a reply to his challenge, lunged at the figure with his rifle and fixed bayonet. To his horror, the long steel bayonet went through the figure with no resistance, and the sentry realised it was a ghost and fainted with terror. Two fellow soldiers testified that they too had seen the ghost, and the sentry was found not guilty.

In 1860, a sentry at the Tower of London saw the ghostly figure of what appeared to be a bear, rising upwards from underneath the Jewel Room door. He issued the usual challenge of 'Who goes there?' Receiving no reply, he attempted to run his bayonet into the figure but there was nothing there. The sentry was so disturbed he lapsed into unconsciousness, and died a few hours later.

The famous Wellington Barracks in London was, at one time, haunted by a female ghost; at the turn of the nineteenth century, a Coldstream Guardsman beheaded his wife, and hoping to avoid discovery, threw her headless body into the canal by the barracks. Her headless ghost haunted the scene of the crime, and Coldstream Guards soldiers on sentry duty swore on oath that they had seen her headless body rise up from the ground in front of their sentry box. Other Guardsmen reported that, whilst on night sentry duty, they heard shrieks and noises from an empty building behind the Armoury House. Cries of 'Bring me a light! Bring me a light!' were heard, though there was no one there. (Courtesy of Peter Underwood)

Stirling Castle, Stirlingshire, is the home base of the Argyll and Sutherland Highlanders, and has a report in the Regimental Log that, in the 1820s, a sentry was found dead on the battlements of the castle. The report states that his relieving sentry, who stated to his officers that the dead man had a look of stark terror on his face, found the man dead at his sentry post. There was no sign of any injury to the dead sentry.

Just after the end of the Second World War, occupants of the castle began to report hearing heavy, measured, slow footsteps on the battlements, as though a sentry was walking his beat. Again, in the 1950s, there were more reports of slow, sentry-like footsteps on the battlements. Nothing was ever found when the battlements were examined. However, the sentry beat on the castle battlements was stopped. Nothing has been heard since of the ghostly footsteps.

Windsor Castle itself has several ghosts. The ancient building was built in 1319, and has a tower named the Curfew Tower, which seems to be the focus of ghostly, slow and dragging footsteps. The tower is situated over the castle dungeons, and has a gruesome history. Prisoners used to be taken to the stairs in the tower to be hanged from a beam 100 feet up from the ground. The unfortunate prisoners' bodies were left hanging as a warning to others. The ghostly, dragging footsteps are those of the prisoners who were hanged.

The ghost of George III looks out on occasion from the room where he once lived, overlooking the parade ground. The king has also been seen in the Royal Library. Modern soldiers have been startled to see him peering out at them from his room, drawn to them by the sound of their drilling and the shouted orders. The poor king liked his soldiers, and loved to see them drilling – he was of course their Commander in Chief!

A Soldier Returns

Like many others, a man from Branscombe, Devon went off to fight for his country during the Second World War. Regretfully, he was killed in

Branscombe, Devon. (*Devon County Council, Rachel Mildon*)

action in Italy in 1944. His widow continued to live in Branscombe, Devon, and was out walking on a beautiful summer's day along a stretch of road between Bovey Cross and Vicarage Hill when she saw a man walking towards her. As he came up to her, she realised that it was her late husband, dressed in his favourite clothes – grey flannel trousers, white shirt, and fawn jacket. He was real and solid. As she looked, the figure disappeared. The war widow was very happy with her experience – perhaps the knowledge that she would see her beloved husband again was consoling, and helped her in her loneliness and grief. (Report from camp barber RAF Chivenor, Devon, 1951)

The United States Capitol and White House Ghosts

Home of United States politicians and lawmakers, the 270-year-old Capitol building, Washington DC is haunted by many ghosts, all representing its history.

Ghostly footsteps of the Capitol Guards can be heard in the corridors of power during the hours of darkness. When a dead illustrious American citizen, of whatever rank, is lying in state on a bier in the Rotunda, a ghostly Unknown Soldier appears to pays his respect to the departed. He approaches the bier, salutes, turns away and disappears.

The White House, home of the President of the United States of America, was built in 1792, and at first was called the President's Palace, until 1901, when it became simply the White House. During the War of 1812, the British did partially burn down the White House, which was saved by a rainstorm which put out the flames. The House has many ghosts, but the military one is a British soldier, who was shot dead by White House guards as he tried to set the White House on fire. The House is called the White House because it was painted white to cover the scorch marks after the British attempt to burn it down.

Channel Island Ghosts of the Second World War

Whilst serving in the Royal Air Force at RAF Fairford, Gloucester, I struck up a friendship with 'Jersey' Cavey, a native of the Channel Islands. During the Second World War, German forces occupied the Islands. On speaking of my interest in the supernatural, he told me of what had happened in the Islands after the Second World War ended, and the Germans left.

On the German long-range gun battery, Mirus, on Guernsey, German soldier ghosts have been seen, covered with blood and ghastly wounds.

It is said that the gun exploded, killing the gun crew who now haunt the place of their death. Other ghostly German soldiers in their field grey uniforms are said to haunt the islands, and the places they were billeted in. Peter Underwood informed me that the Germans employed slave labour to build their defences, and when the defences were finished the slave labourers were killed and their bodies thrown into concrete mixers, then buried in the concrete defences. It has been estimated that some 15,000 bodies were so buried. Their ghosts haunt the still-in existence German defences on Jersey.

Aerial Ghosts and Legends

Owing to the nature of flying, it is inevitable that crashes and collisions will occur; when the author served in the Royal Air force as a regular airman, he was always made aware of the risks of flying, and had to sign that he would serve anywhere in the world, on land, sea and in the air. In the aircrew room, there were posters on the walls, and the one that the author always remembers is 'Isaac Newton is always waiting!' which is a reference to the force of gravity, which is always there, and can destroy an aircraft by ground impact, if it loses its airspeed.

Another feature of service in the Royal Air Force is that legends abound! Gossip and rumour are part of service life. There is the story of the rear-turret air-gunner of a Wellington bomber who, while the engines were running up, prior to moving off the hardstanding, opened his turret, stepped out onto the ground, and walked forward into the fast-revolving three-bladed propeller, driven by the powerful 1,550 hp Bristol engine. He was instantly decapitated. His headless ghost, dressed in Irvin flying gear, haunts RAF Lichfield, Staffordshire, and has been seen by many.

There is the classic Second World War legend that, if a ghostly bomber was seen or heard flying over RAF Lissett, Yorkshire, one or more of the Halifax bombers based there would be shot down or crash, killing all the crew aboard. No one seems to know who or what the ghostly bomber type was: there was no identification. However, it passed into history as the 'Grim Reaper Bomber'.

The greatest number of aerial ghost legends comes from the Lincolnshire area, which was covered with RAF and USAAF airfields during the Second World War. Every airfield has its ghost stories, and haunted control towers are the main focus.

Whist the author was on night duty as Runway Controller at Royal Air Force Station Lyneham, a ground mechanic tyre-checker was killed by stepping backwards into the arc of the revolving port inner propeller of a Hastings transport aircraft, stationary at the end of the main runway, by the author's airfield control caravan. This incident made its way into legend, and is part of the history of RAF Lyneham.

The First World War Ghostly American Airman

During the First World War, the American Army Air Corps sent men and aircraft to Europe to fight against the German Air Service. Many pilots were killed in aerial combat with the more experienced German fighter pilots. On the morning of 19 March 1917, a young woman stationed with her husband in India was putting her baby into its cot when, on some impulse, she looked up and, to her amazement, saw her brother standing by her. She knew that her brother was flying against the Germans in France, and should not be in India. She turned to face her brother, but there was no one there; he had disappeared.

Later, she was told that her brother had been shot down and killed in aerial combat in France at the same moment she had seen him in India. (Courtesy of Martin Caiden)

A Ghostly Explanation

Cardington Royal Airship Works, Bedfordshire, was the home of the British airship. Construction of the massive airship hangar – 700 feet long, 254 feet wide, and 145 feet high – began in 1916, when Shorts Brothers, with a £110,000 loan from the British Government, began design and work on airships.* In early 1917, the Cardington Naval Aircraft Works was opened, but by early 1919 Shorts Brothers had ceased work, and the Admiralty assumed control of the site, now renamed the Royal Airship works.

Four airships were built at Cardington, the first being the R31, in August 1918, then the R32, R37 and R38. Another large airship hangar was built

---

* On a 2008 personal note from the author who enlisted as an RAF regular airman at RAF Cardington in the 1940s: 'I remember being awe-struck at the sight of the massive airship hangars at Cardington. I still have my recruit squad obligatory photograph, taken in front of the hangars! All the RAF buildings are now long gone – but the awesome hangars are still there.'

in 1928, designated No. 2 South Hangar, and intended for long-range airship design and construction.

The R101 airship was 777 feet in length, and designed to carry 100 passengers and forty-eight crew. Her airframe was built at Norwich, and assembled at Cardington's No. 2 South Hangar. She first test-flew on 14 October 1929, but was found to have control handling difficulties.

The giant airship R101 (G-FAAW) took off at 6.36 p.m. on 4 October 1929, from Cardington, Bedfordshire, on the 5,000-mile flight to Karachi, India. As she lifted off, the nose went down, and four tons of water ballast had to be jettisoned to prevent a crash. The airship carried forty-eight crew, plus forty tons of ballast and fuel.

The airship carried several passengers, among them:

> Sir W. Sefton Brancker, KCB, AFC, Director of Civil Aviation.
> Brigadier General the Rt. Hon. Lord Christopher Thomson, CBE, DSO, Secretary of State for Air.
> Squadron Leader William O'Neill, MC, Deputy Director of Civil Aviation, India.
> Major P. Bishop, OBE.
> Squadron Leader W. Palstra, Australian Government.
> Mr James Buck, Valet to Lord Thomson.

British airship R101.

On 5 October 1930, at 2.09 a.m., the R101 crashed in a storm at Beauvais, northern France, and exploded in a ball of five and a half million cubic feet of hydrogen gas, which engulfed the fifty-four passengers, officers, and crew on board, leaving only six survivors: Crewmen Leech, Disley, Binks, Bell, Savory and Cook.

The Director of Civil Aviation, Major-General Sir Sefton Branker, and the airship's Captain, Flight Lieutenant H. Carmichael Irwin, AFC, died in the searing flames. As Irwin died, the telephone switchboard at RAF Cardington showed a call being made from Irwin's office. The night shift operator pushed the telephone call indicator shutter up, but it immediately fell again. The mystified operator pushed up the shutter, but it again fell. With a colleague, the operator checked Irwin's office, but there was no one there. The two operators logged their visit to Irwin's office at 2.07 a.m.

A friend of Branker and Irwin attended two séances (there were seven in all) before the official enquiry was held into the cause of the fatal crash, and recognised the voices of both men giving technical details of the airship and the cause of the crash, which no non-technical person (the medium) could possibly have known. Only a few highly trained airship personnel could have given specific details of the R101's construction, right down to listing number 5-C girder as a possible cause of the fatal crash. Some of the information was highly secret, and known to very few.

The R101's Captain Irvin spoke at length during one séance: 'Cruising speed bad. Ship swinging badly. Engines wrong – too heavy, cannot rise. Never reached cruising altitude'. The second séance had Irwin saying: 'She (the R101) was too heavy by several tons. No lift. Nose strut collapsed, caused rent in cover. Elevator jammed – cannot trim. Impossible to rise.'

The official Court of Enquiry, under Sir John Simon, KC, began on 28 October 1930, and finished on 5 December, 1931. The ghostly evidence from the séances was given to Sir John, but was not used.

The 129-page Enquiry findings were that the R101 crash was due to loss of hydrogen gas due to leakage. There was no mention of the séances and the evidence obtained from them. No mention was made of any girder damage, so structural damage was ruled out.

There was no precedent to admit the ghostly evidence from the airship R101's crew members, no matter how it was obtained!

The Montrose Airfield Ghosts

RAF Montrose, 1 mile north of the town of Montrose, Angus, Scotland, and adjacent to the North Sea Montrose Bay, opened as an RFC training airfield in 1912.

At about 7.25 a.m. on Tuesday, 27 May 1913, Lieutenant Desmond Lucius Arthur, No. 2 Squadron, Royal Flying Corps, took off from Montrose in British Experimental B.E.2 biplane No. 205, built by the Royal Aircraft Factory, and climbed to 2,000 feet; suddenly the upper starboard wing of the biplane cracked, and the aircraft disintegrated around the unfortunate pilot, who had no parachute; he fell out of the aircraft, as there were no safety belts in those days, and plunged to earth, and a violent death. The B.E.2 followed the doomed pilot down, with wings pushed upwards by the downwards thrust. This aircraft was first flown on 12 October 1912 at Larkhill, Wiltshire, but needed a new engine in 1913, so it was fitted with a new 70 hp Renault. Engine failure was not the cause of the fatal crash.

Lieutenant Arthur was accorded a Service funeral with full military honours – all personnel attending the cortege were in full Ceremonial Dress. The tragic airman was interred at Montrose cemetery, after a formal procession through the small town. His resting place is marked by the Service three-stepped cross used at the time – it reads 'Desmond L. Arthur, Lieutenant, Royal Flying Corps, Killed at Montrose, 27 May, 1913'.

The official Board of Enquiry, held by the Accident and Investigation Committee of the Royal Aero Club, found that the wing had not been properly repaired after a prior incident. However, another enquiry by a Government department on 3 August 1916 found that pilot error rather than faulty maintenance was the cause of the B.E.2 disintegrating.

In the autumn of 1916, the figure of a pilot in flying clothing began to appear in the Number 2 Officers' Mess, and was seen by several airmen. A Major Cyril Foggin was walking to the Mess when he saw before him another officer dressed in full flying clothing. Foggin did not recognise the officer in the evening gloom, but he did see him reach the closed Mess door and disappear. Foggin reached the door and opened it – no one was in sight anywhere.

The ghostly pilot appeared then vanished so many times that he became well-known in Royal Flying Corps circles. Major Foggin saw the ghostly officer several more times on the path to the Mess.

A flying instructor was fast asleep in his room one night when something wakened him; he sat up in bed, and saw a man in flying clothing sitting on a chair in the room. The instructor roared at the seated figure, and got out of bed; the seated pilot vanished. It was found that the ghostly pilot only appeared in the old Number 2 Officers' Mess, where Lieutenant Arthur had been billeted.

In 1917, a two man Enquiry Review Board reinstated the original finding of 1913 that the cause of the fatal crash was a damaged wing spar. Their investigation declared, 'It appears probable that the BE2 had been damaged accidentally and that the person or persons responsible for the damage had repaired it as best they could to evade detection and punishment'.

The Montrose ghostly pilot was last seen in January 1917, perhaps satisfied with the findings of the Review Board.

The Second World War broke out, and RAF flying increased at Montrose. In 1940, a Hurricane pilot landing from a combat air interception patrol inexplicably aborted two landings. The third time he landed successfully, and alleged that a biplane had crossed his path as he tried to land. There were no biplanes at RAF Montrose, and the watching ground crew had not seen or heard any other aircraft.

In the summer of 1942, another aircraft crashed at RAF Montrose, killing the Flight Lieutenant pilot. Again, it was alleged that the crash was due to an aircraft fault, not pilot error. A new ghostly pilot, wearing Second World War flying clothing, began appearing at RAF Montrose, seen by many airmen, who nicknamed him 'The Montrose Ghost'. History seemed to be repeating itself. Many new student pilots, who had no knowledge of his alleged existence, saw the ghostly flyer on the Flight Line!

The Second World War ended, and as RAF Montrose wound down, reports of the ghostly pilot decreased until 1946, when the armed Night Camp Patrol were doing their usual security checks, which included the Sick Quarters Mortuary. They had also been told to check an aircraft parked outside the control tower. At 3.00 a.m., after they had checked the locked door of the mortuary, one of the two men had slipped away for a cigarette, leaving one guard by the aircraft. Suddenly there was a loud noise from the mortuary, the locked doors flew open, and a figure rushed out; the figure, dressed in pilots' flying clothing, came towards the guard by the aircraft who saw that his face was as white as chalk. A long bang came from the mortuary as the open doors slammed shut. With the noise, the ghostly pilot disappeared, and the second guard came back from his cigarette-smoking break. He had heard the noise, and wondered what was going on. The other guard kept quiet, and did not mention the ghostly pilot coming towards the aircraft.

Some years later, at another RAF station, the guard who had seen the Montrose ghost leave the mortuary and vanish was talking to another airman, who had also been stationed at Montrose. The conversation came round to the Montrose ghosts, and the airman told the guard that, in 1942, a Flight Lieutenant pilot had come out of the then Operations Room by kicking open the door in a temper, and marched to his aircraft near the control tower. The bad-tempered pilot took off, but crashed on take-off, with fatal results. It appeared that the Operations Room later became the mortuary! That was why the ghostly pilot came out from the mortuary, which he still thought was the Operations Room!

On 27 May 1963, Sir Peter Masefield, Chairman of the then British Overseas Airways Corporation (BOAC), was flying his personal Chipmunk aircraft from Dalcross (Inverness), Scotland, en route to Shoreham, Sussex, when his flight plan route brought him close to Montrose airfield. Sir Peter had flown from Montrose before, and recognised the three Somerfield track runways, and the Montrose Bay seashore. Flying at 2,500 feet above the seashore, he saw ahead of his aircraft a biplane aircraft; closing rapidly on the biplane, he identified it as a First World War B.E.2 trainer! Still closing, Sir Peter flew alongside, and saw the pilot was wearing a leather helmet, and a long scarf. Astounded and mystified, Sir Peter saw the outer part of the B.E.2's upper right wing begin to break up, with the entire wing section flapping and wrenching itself from its struts. The leather-coated pilot fell from the doomed aircraft, as the B.E.2 went out of control and fell spinning onto Montrose airfield.

Sir Peter landed on an adjacent golf course, and called to some players to come to the airfield crash site. When they arrived on the airfield, there was no wreckage; there was nothing in sight.

It was almost fifty years to the day, 27 May 1913, that Lieutenant Arthur, flying a B.E.2, died over Montrose Airfield in exactly the same way that Sir Peter had seen on 27 May 1963.

RAF Montrose finally closed down in as an airfield in 1980 to be used by industry; there are no known reports of the Montrose Ghosts being seen since.

The Ghostly Flying Duchess

The summer house at Woburn Abbey, Bedfordshire, is believed to be haunted by the spirit of the Duke of Bedford's grandmother, a famous, intrepid pilot known as the Flying Duchess, who died in an aircraft crash in the sea off Norfolk on 22 March 1937, after taking off solo from the Abbey in her De Havilland Gipsy Moth, identification letters G-ACUR. There is a stained-glass memorial in the Abbey to the memory of the Duchess.

RAF Drem – A Ghostly Airfield out of Time

RAF Drem, some 4 miles north-north-west of Haddington, East Lothian, Scotland, opened as a grass airfield in 1917. It was closed in 1919, at the end of the First World War, but reopened in 1939 as a flying training station with No. 13 Flying Training School, complete with bright, yellow-painted aircraft in occupation (training aircraft were and are painted yellow to show they are trainers and let other aircraft beware). A month later, fighter aircraft began to arrive, and Drem was a fighter base for the rest of the Second World War.

Drem's main claim to fame is that the Air Ministry devised the RAF Airfield Lighting Mark 1 there, and it became known as the Drem system.

In 1935, some years before the Second World War erupted, a regular Royal Air Force pilot was flying in heavy stratus cloud over East Lothian. Trying to find his bearings, he flew lower to get beneath the cloud. The pilot knew the East Lothian area, as he had been there before. Looking out of his cockpit, he saw an airfield ahead, which he identified as Drem, which he had visited the day before. He knew Drem was disused and in need of repair, and given to agriculture – farm animals were used to keep the grass short.

Suddenly, his aircraft was out of cloud and in brilliant sunshine over Drem airfield. But it was not the Drem airfield he had seen the day before! This one was immaculate, with three bright yellow (yellow is the standard RAF flying training aircraft colour, adopted in about 1938) Avro 504N fighters, and one Miles Magister training aircraft lined up in front of open hangar doors. As the pilot flew his aircraft over Drem, he saw RAF flight mechanics dressed in blue overalls pushing out another aircraft. By this time, the pilot had to pull back on the stick, and open the throttle to pull up over the hangars. He knew that the airmen below would look up because of the noise of his aircraft's engine – none did! In seconds, the aircraft was pulling away from Drem, but not before the pilot saw the whole grass airfield had neatly cut grass, with no farm animals grazing.

Leaving Drem, the aircraft was immediately back in stratus cloud, and the pilot climbed to above cloud level. Setting course for his base in southern England, the pilot realised that the Drem airfield he had just seen was not the Drem airfield he had seen the day before – that was derelict, with animals grazing on the grass. Also, RAF aircraft in 1935 were not painted training yellow, and RAF mechanics wore brown overalls, not blue.

The pilot landed at his base, and related his experience to his fellow Wing Commanders – none believed him! It would appear that the pilot had time-slipped from the derelict Drem airfield into the future Drem airfield.

Ghostly Spitfires and Airmen

Biggin Hill, Kent, perhaps the most famous Second World War RAF 11 Group fighter airfield, was first opened in 1917 as a Royal Flying Corps airfield, and played a decisive part in the 1940 Battle of Britain. Victorious Spitfire and Hurricane fighter pilots did a victory roll over the airfield after returning from a sortie if they had shot down an enemy aircraft. The German Luftwaffe knew Biggin Hill was important as a Spitfire airfield, and bombed it to try and take it out of action. 453 aircrew were lost flying out of Biggin Hill, and their names are inscribed on the altar reredos, and on four stained-glass windows of the St George's Chapel at the airfield.

Although the airfield is still in use, fighter aircraft have long disappeared from it, but it is said by a group of former Royal Air Force fighter pilots, who held a reunion at their old wartime airfield, that a lone, ghostly Spitfire can sometimes be seen and heard roaring over the airfield, with the unmistakable sound of the famous Merlin engine at full throttle, do a victory roll, then disappear. The ghostly Spitfire is usually seen and heard on a warm summer's evening; some observers say they can see the unmistakeable shape of the famous fighter aircraft.

The sounds of bombing have been heard, and the sound of an aircraft falling earthwards, then crashing in an explosion. Ghostly aircrew in flying clothing have been seen, walking along runway QDM 215. Are they some of the 453 aircrew who lost their lives during the Second World War?

In the Officers' Mess, the ghost of a Pilot Officer in flying clothing who died in an air crash on 17 September 1941 is said to stand on the staircase of the Mess, looking out towards the spot where he died.

In 1940, a Second World War 604 Squadron Spitfire crashed, on landing, into a RAF standard barrack block, at what was RAF Hendon, during the Battle of Britain, killing the pilot. Over the years, a ghostly pilot wearing Second World War-issue flying clothing: Irvin flying jacket, flying boots, silk polka-dot scarf (worn by fighter pilots to prevent 'weavers neck', causing by constant turning of the head to prevent their being bounced by opposing enemy aircraft), and carrying a pipe, has been seen near a ghostly parked Spitfire outside the barracks block, and inside, in a corridor (without his Spitfire)! The lingering smell of pipe tobacco smoke is often smelt.

The RAF Museum stands near the RAF Hendon airfield site, which was opened in 1910. It has the ghost of a dead airman, who is said to have crashed his B.E.2c biplane into a tree between the old, original hangars.

At the former Second World War RAF Kenley airfield, a ghostly Spitfire comes in on finals (final landing approach), crashes, bursts into flames, and vanishes.

Again in Kent, Royal Air Force Station Hawkinge, 2 miles from Folkestone, opened in 1915 as an airfield. During the Second World War, when the airfield was a forward airfield of 11 Group, Fighter Command, the airfield came under attack by Hitler's first V (Victory) weapon, the V1 unmanned Flying Bomb, which caused many casualties when it fell and its one ton warhead exploded. RAF Hawkinge closed in 1962, and was given up to housing. Thirty-three years later, local people say they heard again the distinctive note of the single jet engine of a V1 Flying Bomb flying overhead.

Royal Air Force Station, Hibaldstow, Lincolnshire, opened in May 1941 as a 12 Group, Fighter Command three-runway tarmac airfield. It closed in 1945. In 1953, a group of former fighter pilots returned to the now disused airfield, rotting away, with long grass covering where the runways had been, on a nostalgic visit. They lingered for an hour, exchanging wartime stories, and then began to walk back to their cars. As they reached their cars, they turned to take one last long look at their old base; as they stared at where the main runway had been, they heard the sound of a Merlin aircraft engine being throttled back for landing. In amazement, they saw a Mark IV Spitfire coming in over the main runway, undershoot, and float down for a perfect landing. As the Spitfire reached the airfield perimeter, it abruptly vanished before their eyes.

Royal Air Force Station, Ouston, 1 mile south of Stamfordham, Durham, opened as a 12 Fighter Group airfield in 1941. Its main function was as an Operational Training Unit (OTU), training fighter pilots. Thirteen RAF Squadrons used the airfield during the Second World War.

The airfield developed tales of the Station Sick Bay being haunted, with Sick Bay staff reporting that lights have been switched on and off without human hands operating them. The Sick Bay main door was locked at night, but every night it was found open; the key was kept in the Station Guard Room, but it made no difference. The locked door was opened without a key. Airmen sleeping in Nissen huts near the Sick Bay were woken up during the night by unexplained loud noises and heavy footsteps. These were believed to be connected to a pilot who had been killed near the Sick Bay, to where his body had been taken.

Parachute Drop Ghosts

RAF Henlow, Bedfordshire, opened as a Maintenance Command airfield in 1918. In the early 1930s, it was an aircraft depot, with several hangars housing aircraft and spare parts. In accordance with RAF procedure, the complex was patrolled by airmen on Camp Patrol, armed with pickaxe handles. (The author remembers doing this patrol very well!)

Airmen underwent parachute static line training at Henlow, in which the parachute strop, being attached to a static line in the aircraft, opened the parachute.

An airman on a jump jumped, but his parachute went into a 'Roman Candle' (the parachute failed to develop, usually by faulty packing). As he fell earthwards, he was screaming in abject terror of an imminent death. He died on impact with the ground.

Airmen on night camp patrol began to report hearing terrified screams, as though the dead airman was still falling to the ground in terror.

On a disused airfield on the Isle of Wight, several ex-Royal Air Force personnel were visiting their former base when they saw a figure on a parachute descending. All craned their necks to see who was parachuting down; there was no sound of any aircraft in the area. As the figure on the parachute dropped earthwards, they were horrified to see that the figure had no head. As they watched, the parachutist's feet touched the ground, and the figure vanished. Making enquiries of local people in the pub, they were told that the headless figure on the parachute had been seen many times – no one knows who it is.

The Sick Quarters' Ghostly Orderly

Royal Air Force, Bletchley had, like most RAF Stations, a Station Sick Quarters, where Service patients were admitted when ill with minor ailments. The RAF Camp was in use during the Second World War as part of a code-breaking team. As most of the service personnel were young and fit, the wards were barely used. Several patient airmen reported to the medical staff that they had seen the ghostly figure of a nurse, dressed in a green apron and pushing a trolley laid out with surgical instruments through the wards during the hours of darkness. As the green-apron-wearing ghostly figure reached the end of the ward, it disappeared. After the war, the station was demolished, and there have been no more reports of the ghostly orderly.

The RAF Barrack Room Ghost and Tales of the Writer

RAF Netheravon, 16 miles north of Salisbury, Wiltshire, began life at the end of 1912, when the Air Battalion, Royal Engineers, took over some Army Cavalry School buildings (where my wife's male family served, rode

The author outside the hut at RAF Netheravon, sixty years after he saw a ghost there.

and worked), on a stretch of high ground, uphill from Netheravon village. Two grass air landing areas were laid out, designated North and South Airfields. On 16 June 1913, No. 3 Squadron RFC moved in to Netheravon, and the airfield filled with aircraft. Construction of Messes, hangars and other necessary buildings began to First World War specification. The airmen's living quarters were grouped round the parade ground, with the Officers' and Sergeants' Messes nearby.

The author – then an eighteen-year-old airman – was posted to RAF Netheravon in the 1940s, and allocated a barrack room bed space in one of the wooden huts immediately on the edge of the airfield. Ten other airmen were billeted in the same hut, all of the same age. Being young, fit airmen all slept well in the comfortable billet, but were accustomed to being awakened at short notice for duty. One night, I was fast asleep in my bed, when I awoke for no reason. The room was dark, but with night vision it was easy to see the whole room without putting on the lights. Standing at the bottom of my bed was a dark figure dressed in First World War flying clothing of a primitive nature. I sat up in bed and stared at the figure. It did not move. I was not afraid. Being young, fit and unafraid of anything I roared expletives at the figure, which, perhaps startled at my aggressive behaviour, moved and faded away! Bedlam broke out as the other airmen awoke, but promptly went back to sleep when I said I had seen a ghost! Rude words were hurled in my direction. I went back to sleep.

Sixty years later, I returned with my family to pay a nostalgic visit to Netheravon airfield. I had a conducted tour by a security guard named Bob, but my tour was confusing; the airfield as I had known it was gone. However, Bob took me to the old wooden huts where we had slept and lived in, and I wondered if the First World War ghostly airman still haunted my hut.

The Control Tower Ghosts

RAF Linton on Ouse, 9 miles north-west of York, opened as a three runway Bomber Command airfield in 1937, with thirty-six heavy bombers, hardstanding dispersals and a flying control tower. During the Second World War, it was an important operational bomber base, with the main Runway 22 much in use. Post-Second World War, the airfield continued in use as an RAF base.

During 1959, Warrant Officer Walter Hodgson, one of the gallant aircrew survivors who flew out of Linton on Ouse during the Second World War, died at a young age, and his ashes were scattered along Runway 22, whence he had often flown. The placing of a memorial plaque near the control tower marked the decorated hero, his life and times. In the late summer of 1988, the memorial plaque was moved from outside to inside the control tower. Members of the control room staff saw, coincidental with the moving of the plaque, the figure of a Second World War airman in flying clothing, the grey figure appearing then vanishing.

It was deduced that the grey figure was that of the dead RAF hero, who did not like his memorial plaque moved. His family were contacted, and assured the staff that there was no need to be afraid of the gallant airman who had passed away. There were no more sightings. (Courtesy of Martin Caiden)

RAF East Kirby was situated 4 miles south-west of Spilsby, Lincolnshire, opened in 1943 as a three-runway Bomber Command airfield, and closed in 1970. The flying control tower (all formerly called watch towers until the universal introduction of radio telephones – R/T) is reputed to be haunted by the figure of a United States Army Air Force officer wearing a Second World War A-2 flying jacket. Legend has it that the air force officer is a crew member of a B-17G Flying Fortress, which crashed while attempting to land in December 1944, killing all ten crew.

Croydon Airfield Ghosts

Croydon airfield, Surrey, 11 miles south of London, opened as an airfield in 1916, during the First World War, and hosted some of the most illustrious squadrons of the Royal Air Force before closing in 1955, and being turned over to housing. In 1928, the airfield became London International Airport, Croydon, but was replaced in 1955 by Gatwick.

Twenty-two RAF Squadrons in total flew from and to the airfield (Nos 1, 2, 3, 17, 32, 41, 72, 84, 92, 111, 116, 115, 147, 207, 271,287, 302, 307, 501, 605, 607 and 615). During the Second World War, Croydon airfield was attacked by the German Luftwaffe during the Battle of Britain when 111 Hurricane Squadron was in occupation, causing eighty casualties.

The housing development on what had been the three grass runways got into full swing, but sure enough, tales of ghostly airmen began to emerge.

On the site of the Second World War Officers' Mess, men singing wartime songs have been heard; the site had taken a direct hit, and all inside had bought it (been killed). On Mollison Drive, a headless motorcyclist has been seen: the ghost of an airman killed during an air raid. A Luftwaffe pilot wearing standard German Luftwaffe flying clothing has been seen in one of the old hangars; he is reputed to be the dead crewmember of a German aircraft shot down over Croydon airfield.

In the late 1970s, a young couple moved into one of the recently-built houses. The wife was in the bedroom, dressing to go out, when she saw the figure of a Second World War pilot in the room. He was dressed in an RAF-issue Irvin leather, sheepskin-lined, flying jacket, suede flying boots and wearing a leather flying helmet with goggles and oxygen mask. The ghostly pilot disappeared then reappeared three more times – once when the man and wife were together.

The husband was a collector of militaria, and bought a Second World War German SS uniform on a tailor's dummy. The black-uniformed, infamous SS (*Schutzstaffel–Squad*) was feared throughout Europe for their conduct during the war. The uniformed dummy was placed in the hallway of the couple's home, but the now-invisible pilot ghost threw the dummy and its hated uniform across the hall. Later, the ghostly pilot came into the couple's spare bedroom, where another couple was sleeping; in the small hours of the night, when the husband was using the toilet, the visiting wife felt the bedclothes being torn from the bed and flung on the bedroom floor.

The owners of the house decided to turn to the Church, and a local priest conducted an exorcism. During the religious ceremony, the wife felt a hand on the strap of her bra, which was pulled – no one at the ceremony was near her!

It would appear that the ghostly pilot – still clad in his flying clothing – objected to the notorious SS uniform being on his airfield!

Three Aircrew Ghosts at Bircham Newton

RAF Bircham Newton, Norfolk, was built in 1916, and used as a Training Station. It has a claim to fame, in that it was chosen to be the first base of RAF long-range bombers – Handley Page V/1500 four-engined aircraft, built to deliver bombs on Berlin during the First World War. The Armistice came before the bombers were due to be ordered to bomb Berlin.

The airfield had no permanent tarmac runways; instead, it had three steel matting-track runways, but it did have extensive technical and domestic buildings, with the Squash Racquets Court built to Air Ministry Specification 2078 /1918. During the Second World War, it was used mainly by Coastal Command of 16 Group. Maximum strength of RAF personnel during the Second World War was 2,431, with another 554 WAAFs. Thirty-nine squadrons used the busy airfield.

Bircham Newton closed as a RAF Station on 18 December 1962, and was taken over as the Construction Industry Training Centre (CITC). The three C-Type aircraft hangars remained, as did many of the old buildings.

Film Crews often use the site for Building Industry Training Films, and on one occasion a film crewmember decided to use the old squash court built in 1918. Playing on his own, with no one else on, or in, the court he heard a noise, and turned round; behind him in the viewing gallery was the figure of a man, dressed in RAF uniform, glaring at him, before vanishing abruptly.

The film crew placed a tape recorder in the court building, and left it running when they left. On playing back the tape later, they heard strange sounds for an empty building: human voices talking, aircraft being serviced with 2nd Line servicing cranes and pulleys, and other unidentifiable sounds.

A séance was held in the squash court, and a dead airman contacted the medium. It transpired that an airman had committed suicide during its war-time years. Staff at the airfield told of various hauntings over the years they had worked there: poltergeist activity, throwing off bedclothes and causing mayhem, figures in RAF uniform which disappeared without trace.

Another television team investigated, and enrolled two experienced mediums to assist their enquiries. The Mediums found that there was the ghost of an airman in the squash court. One medium made contact with the dead airman, who said that he and two other aircrew had been killed in a plane crash at Bircham Newton, behind the local village church.

It transpired during the séance that the three aircrew had been squash players, and had used the haunted squash court. It is reported that the three made an agreement that if they were killed in action or flying, they would meet again in the squash court.

The mediums read an exorcism in the squash court to lay the spirits of the three dead airmen, and allow them to pass over in peace.

The Intelligence Officer's Ghosts

Michael Bentine, the BBC *Goon Show* comic, was a RAF Intelligence Officer during the Second World War, and has written on his service in briefing and debriefing aircrew, before and after raids on Germany. At one briefing, before aircraft take-off, he looked into the face of the airman before him, and instead of a face he saw a skull. Bentine knew that this airman would not return from his raid over Germany. Sadly, the airman did not return.

Bentine was Intelligence Officer at RAF Wickenby, a No. 1 Group, Bomber Command airfield, 9 miles north of Lincoln, during the harsh winter of 1943-1944. He had as an oppo (RAF term for a close friend) a fellow Flight Lieutenant, who had finished a full thirty-mission tour of bombing operations. Bentine went go on a '48' (forty-eight-hour Saturday and Sunday weekend pass (called in RAF slang a '48' or '295')), and before he went, he said goodbye to his oppo.

Bentine returned late on Sunday night – his '48' expired at 11.59 p.m. Sunday – and found RAF Wickenby covered in snow, which showed up all the Nissen corrugated huts which served as sleeping quarters for all ranks due to wartime shortages. As Bentine walked to his billet, he saw his oppo walking in the snow, some 40 feet across his path, heading for his own Nissen hut. Bentine called out a greeting, which his oppo returned before disappearing. The next day, Bentine was told that his oppo had been killed in an air crash, twenty-four hours before Bentine had seen and spoken to him, late on Sunday night.

The Lindholme Airmen Ghosts

RAF Lindholme, 7 miles east-north-east of Doncaster, began life in 1938/1940 as a No. 5 Group bomber airfield, with two runways and thirty-six heavy hardstandings. It was only 20 feet above sea level, with Lindholme Lake 3 miles east, and marsh bogs at the end of one runway. The last RAF usage was in 1978. At present it is HM Prison, Lindholme.

On 20 July 1941, No. 305 Polish ('Weilkoposki') Squadron moved into RAF Lindholme, and equipped with Vickers Wellington 1C aircraft. The squadron commenced night bombing raids into the Ruhr valley of Germany, which continued until August 1943, when it transferred to day bombing.

After a bombing raid over Cologne, a Wellington overshot runway 232 and sank out of sight in the peat bog; none of the aircrew were found.

Second World War legend has it that a badly damaged, Polish-piloted Wellington bomber, returning one night from bombing Germany, had a badly wounded sergeant pilot who ordered his aircrew to bale out, whilst he attempted to land the stricken bomber. The aircrew baled out, leaving the pilot alone. The Wellington aircraft came down in Lindholme Bog, and disappeared beneath the surface.

Three weeks or so later, the Station Padre was on the airfield at night, when he saw a blood-stained figure in Second World War flying clothing approaching. The figure said, 'Sir, can you direct me to the Sergeants' Mess?' in a strong Polish accent. The padre pointed to the nearby Sergeants' Mess, and the figure walked away into the darkness before the Padre could offer assistance.

The wounded Sergeant pilot was seen by others at Lindholme airfield, and on one occasion spoke to the Station Commander Group Captain, asking the same question. As the figure disappeared, the Group Captain ordered a search of the area, but nothing was found.

The Second World War ended, but on numerous occasions the ghostly, wounded Sergeant pilot kept appearing at Lindholme, still asking the same question, and always disappearing. He came to be known as 'Lindholme Willy'.

One version of the legend has it that the bomber crashed into the bog, killing all but the wounded pilot, who managed to stagger from the aircraft – in the bog – and die on the doorstep of the Sergeants' Mess.

Another version is that the ghost seen is that of William Bland, who lived in Lindholme Bog as a hermit in 1620, and whose ghost took the form of an airman during the Second World War!

Other legends abound about the Lindholme ghostly airman/airmen – one has it that there is a Hampden light bomber still down in the bog, with the dead aircrew aboard. Handley Page Hampdens, aircraft of 50 Squadron, were based at Lindholme, and took part on the first RAF bombing raid on Berlin, on the night of 25/26 August 1940.

In 1975, Fisons Fertiliser Company dredged Lindholme Bog, known as Hatfield Waste, for peat, and found the wreckage of a crashed Wellington aircraft, identified from its geodetic construction. In the cockpit were four unidentifiable human remains. A Wellington aircraft carried five aircrew.

The remains were removed, and the RAF authorities informed. A funeral with full RAF Military Honours was accorded, and the remains interred in Lindholme Churchyard.

On 23 July 1987 a Fison's workman, digging for peat, found the peat-preserved body of a Polish airman, which bore injuries consistent to him falling from an aircraft at height. The airman's body could not be identified. He was buried on 11 November 1987, at RAF Finningley.

The Honington Airfield Ghost

RAF Honington lies 7 miles north of Bury St Edmunds, Suffolk, and became part of RAF Transport Command in 1946; as such, it was a regular run from RAF Upper Heyford, Oxfordshire, where I was stationed. In July 1948, I flew, in Dakota A for Able, from Heyford to Honington. The usual hospitality was forthcoming, and I was told of the Station ghost. It appears that an aircraft returning from a mission over Germany during the Second World War caught fire in the circuit. The pilot baled out, but fell onto the top of a hangar. Unbelievably, in spite of a horrendous impact, he made his way down to ground level, and walked away. A few seconds later he collapsed. The Station Medical Crew went to his aid, but he was dead. His ghost is said to re-enact his fall and death at intervals.

The Dambusters Ghost

The famous RAF 617 (Special Duties) Squadron was formed on 21 March 1943 at RAF Scampton, Lincolnshire, primarily for one specific operation:

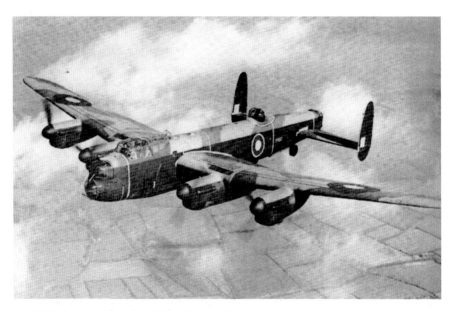

An RAF Lancaster bomber. (*Chris Bowyer*)

Operation Downwood, the breaching of the Mohne, Eder and Sorpe dams in the Ruhr, Germany, using Barnes Wallis's immense bouncing bombs, filled with 6,000 lb of RDX explosive. These were to be carried in adapted Lancaster heavy bombers.

Operation Downwood began on the night of 16-17 May 1943, when nineteen Lancasters, led by Wing Commander Guy Gibson, took off from RAF Scampton, and set course for the Ruhr. One of the Lancasters, codenamed Z for Zebra, was flown by a 617 Squadron Flight Commander, Squadron Leader Henry Maudslay, DFC.

Over the Eder Dam, Gibson, using plain language over the R/T, said to Maudslay, 'Hello, Z Zebra you have a go now'. Maudslay replied, 'Roger – Wilco', and dived to the attack. Flying very low over the water, Z Zebra dropped its bouncing bomb right on the parapet. The 6,000 lb of RDX explosive bomb went off, and blew Z Zebra out of existence – killing all on board instantly.

Guy Gibson saw Z Zebra blown to pieces, but for some unknown reason called on the R/T 'Henry – Henry, Z Zebra – Z Zebra are you all right?' There was no reply, only the mush of the R/T. Gibson called again; this time, there was a faint reply, 'I think so – stand by'.

All the surviving Lancaster aircrews on the Squadron open R/T channel heard the reply from Z Zebra. All knew that Z Zebra had disintegrated in the bouncing bomb blast. Nothing was ever heard of, or wreckage found, of Z Zebra. She had disappeared from existence. Or had she?

On 20 September 1944, Wing Commander Guy Gibson, VC, DSO & Bar, DFC & Bar, died in a Mosquito XX of 627 Squadron over Holland whilst returning from a raid on Germany. His ghost is, or rather was, said to haunt the Second World War control tower at RAF Scampton, where a WAAF Flying Control Assistant saw it. He and his dead 617 Squadron crews are also reported to haunt the Petwood Hotel, Woodhall Spa, which was used as an Officers' Mess during the Second World War. Noises, said to be airmen playing Mess Rugger, and singing old wartime songs, come from what was the squadron bar. Guy Gibson is often seen, dressed in blue RAF uniform, walking towards what is now the 'Lancaster Bar'.

Guy Gibson's black Labrador dog, 'Nigger', was run over and killed, just before 617 Squadron took off on the Dams raid. Gibson asked his Senior NCO, Flight Sergeant Powell, to bury the dog outside the squadron office at midnight, when 617 would be over Germany. Many airmen running around RAF Scampton have seen the ghost of a black Labrador dog. It frequents the Officers' Mess and the fields outside, running soundlessly, as though looking for someone. 'Nigger' is still looking for his master, Guy Gibson.

The Möhne Dam bust!

In Derbyshire's Derwent valley lies the Ladybower reservoir, part of the Derwent Dams system, built in 1916. It was there that 617 Squadron, in training for their epic Dam Busters raid in 1943, practised low-level precise bombing runs in their Lancaster aircraft.

No Lancaster aircraft were lost during the low-level training sorties, but a ghostly Lancaster has often been seen flying, but not heard, over the dam. The phantom Lancaster flies during the day or night, with all four powerful Merlin engines running, and the propellers turning, but making no noise. Is this Lancaster Z for Zebra, flown by Squadron Leader Maudslay, still making practice sorties over the reservoir that many people have seen? Every year, police in the area have reports from members of the public that they have seen aircraft 'crashing'. No aircraft are ever found by searchers. A ghostly airman dressed in First World War flying clothing (airmen of this era wore motorcycle clothing; there was no issue flying clothing) was seen coming out of the dam waters and walking over the ground, then disappearing into a wood.

The Ghostly Second World War Wellington Bomber

The famous Vickers Wellington twin-engine night bomber first flew in 1932, and was universally known as the 'Wimpey'. It was the backbone of Bomber Command's night bomber assault on Germany during the early part of the Second World War. During the war, 11,461 Wellingtons were produced, the last being delivered on 13 October 1945. Ninety-eight squadrons of the Royal Air Force, some of which used what is now the Brecon Beacons National Park as a flying training area, used the Wellington aircraft.

On the western edge of the Welsh Brecon Beacons National Park lies the valley of the River Tywi and it is here, near the town of Llandeilo, that a ghostly Wellington bomber has been seen flying low in daylight, on several occasions. The sturdy aircraft, which had two Bristol Pegasus 1,000 hp, or Hercules 1,500 hp engines fitted, makes no noise, although the two propellers are turning at high revolutions, at fine pitch. Its passage through the air makes a silent slipstream. There are no Vickers Wellington bombers now flying, anywhere in the world. (Courtesy of Peter Underwood)

Ghostly Music and Second World War Songs

Around the British Isles, ghostly airmen still frequent their Second World War pubs. The Pheasant near Middle Wallop, Hampshire, and the Black Bull, Welton, Lincolnshire, are known examples.

Some of RAF Biggin Hill's billets still stand along with other buildings, and it is said by locals that the sounds of young men singing Second World War songs can be heard on a cold, still night. The original Operations Block at Biggin Hill is reputed to be haunted.

RAF Bourn, Cambridgeshire, was opened in 1941 as an 8 (Bomber Command) Group airfield, staffed by 1,827 airmen and 234 airwomen. Wartime casualties were high, and Major Glen Miller's Army Air Force Band is said to be heard playing all the famous hits, 'American Patrol', 'String of Pearls', 'Moonlight Serenade', and so on. His music, and the sound of young voices singing, are said to come from the site of the old airfield. RAF Bourn was returned to agriculture in 1948.

RAF Helmswell, 7 miles east of Gainsborough, Lincolnshire, was a three-runway First World War airfield, which closed in 1919, and reopened in 1937 as a No.1 Bomber Group base, with a 2,582-strong staff. Many casualties were suffered by airmen – there is a memorial to 170 Squadron on the airfield, to those who died. The bomber airfield closed in 1967. Both First World War and Second World War dance-band music is heard coming from where the old airfield was – Glen Miller seems to be the favourite. Aircraft engines running up (testing their engines) can be heard in the dark, prior to an air test before taking off to bomb Germany. On one ghostly occasion, an old military aircraft landed, and the sounds of the Duty Crew going out to it in a Crew Bus were heard. As they did so, the airfield landing lights were switched on in a blaze of colours, sodium yellow for the runway, blue for the perimeter track, and red for obstructions and end of runway. Suddenly silence, and all sounds and lights vanished.

The American Military Hospital at Odstock, south of Salisbury, was built just before D-Day, 1944. Its purpose was to care for American Servicemen wounded in action on D-Day and afterwards. Another such hospital was built at St Ives, Ringwood, Hampshire.

Both hospitals performed magnificently until the Second World War ended, when the American Government donated both temporary hospitals to Britain. The cash-strapped Government accepted the donations with alacrity; there was only one Hospital in Salisbury – the Infirmary!

The old wartime buildings were adapted for civilian use by installing up-to-date improvements. The long corridors were draught-proofed with plastic doors which, as the author remembers, were not draught proof!

I visited the hospital many times, as my relatives were patients there, and was told by staff of the sounds of music and rowdy parties during the night from near Woodford Ward. I said this was unusual in a hospital, and my informant Brian said 'Oh, it's the Americans who died after D-Day. They are heard singing from time to time. Nothing to worry about.'

Syrencoat House. Headquarters for Airborne Forces and RAF 38 Group during the Second World War, it was codenamed Broadmoor but known as 'The Madhouse'.

The Paratroop Ghost at Syrencot House, Wiltshire

The old Georgian Syrencot House, Brigmerston, on the back road from RAF Netheravon and the Army base at Bulford, Wiltshire, was chosen in 1942 as the combined headquarters of 1st Airborne Division and Royal Air Force (Airborne Forces) Group. There, the detailed planning for D-Day, 6 June 1944, was carried out. The house's code name was 'Broadmoor', but the staff there called it 'The Madhouse'.

One of the civilian staff was Mrs Margaret Besant (the author's mother-in-law), who told the author on many occasions that she had seen a male paratrooper ghost in the house's kitchen. Questioned at length, she gave a graphic description of a paratrooper wearing a Dennison camouflaged smock, red beret, denim trousers, gaiters and army boots. He usually appeared in the kitchen late in the evening, when it was quiet, and walked noiselessly to and fro, without looking at her. Mrs Besant was not frightened, as the ghost always disappeared abruptly. Who the ghost is, or was, no one knows. The house is now the base of a local construction company.

The Stanton Harcourt Ghost

Ex-RAF airman Maurice Harris, an elderly neighbour of the author, was stationed at RAF Stanton Harcourt, 5½ miles west of Oxford, during the Second World War, and up to a few years ago attended reunions there. He tells of his Second World War time there, and I found the following interesting.

RAF Stanton Harcourt was a satellite of 91 Group, RAF Abingdon, designated as No. 10 Bomber Operational Training Unit (OTU), and opening in 1940. It closed in 1946, and reverted to agriculture and gravel extraction. However, as is usual due to its strong construction, the wartime Type 12779/41 flying control tower still stands where it was built. Local superstition has it that the ghost of a young RAF pilot, dressed in Second World War flying kit haunts the old control tower. He is reputed to be that of a pilot killed in a training accident during the War.

The Ghostly Spitfire Pilot

RAF North Weald, 2½ miles north-east of Epping, Essex, was first opened in 1916, and was one of only nine RAF airfields which had two runways, one 1,600 x 50 yards, and one of 1,400 x 50 yards, built of tarmac and wood chippings. In 1940, it was in the front line in defending England against the German Luftwaffe, with seven fighter squadrons under the command of Fighter Command, and 11 Group, Uxbridge.

By late September, the Battle of Britain had been won by the Royal Air Force against the numerically-superior Luftwaffe, but sporadic action continued over the south of England and the English Channel. One squadron took off to intercept German aircraft, and a vicious dogfight developed. The Luftwaffe retreated and the Spitfires made for North Weald. One Spitfire was badly shot up by German fire, and lagged behind the squadron heading for their home base. As the bullet-riddled Spitfire staggered into the North Weald circuit, the Flying Control Officer (Second World War name for air traffic control) tried to contact the stricken aircraft on 117.9 mega cycles R/T without success. Guessing that the aircraft's radio was out of action, the Controller broadcast to the pilot, in the hope that he could hear, to pancake the Spitfire anywhere on the airfield. As the Spitfire turned on finals (final approach) with his undercarriage retracted, he chose to land on the grass, to avoid sparks from the fuselage igniting the Merlin engine's high octane fuel. Suddenly, the aircraft struck a hump in the grass, did a ground loop, turned over then burst into flames. The Airfield Crash crews were on the scene in seconds, and pulled the badly wounded but conscious pilot from the flames. As he was placed in the Crash Crew tender, he insisted on being taken to the Operations Room to be debriefed. The Station Medical Officer attended as best he could to the wounded pilot, who insisted that he call the de-briefing officer at once. The Medical Officer did as was requested by the pilot and left the room. Just as the Medical Officer left the room and had taken but a few steps, he heard the sound of dragging footsteps on the wooden floor, then a loud thump. Both the officers rushed into the Operations Room, and saw the wounded pilot lying dead on the floor. Next to his hand was a telephone, with the cord hanging off the telephone receiver. The dead pilot, even though he was mortally wounded, had tried to make a last telephone call – perhaps to a loved one.

The staff at North Weald, usually on night duty, began to report that they heard dragging footsteps and a heavy thump from the Operations room when they were on duty. When they entered the room, there was the telephone hanging off the hook. Replacing the telephone on the receiver, they again heard the sounds of dragging feet and a heavy thump; entering the room again, they saw the telephone was off the hook again ...

Over the years, till North Weald closed and was returned to industrial use, the same sounds of feet dragging on the wooden floor, and the heavy thump of the pilot's body falling to the ground, were heard again and again, until the Operations Room and block were demolished.

The Ghost of Manfred Von Richthofen - The Red Baron

The German Luftwaffe had been beaten in the Battle of Britain in 1940, and they now turned their attention to night-bombing London and the south of England with bombers. The Royal Air Force responded by training their fighter aircrew in night fighting. The first part of the training was to send airmen in their Hurricanes and Spitfires into the night sky, and fly along the English Channel coast at night to intercept the incoming Luftwaffe bombers based in France.

One young fighter pilot was sent on a sortie over Dover so he could keep his bearings in visual flight conditions (VFR), when he saw ahead of him the dim glow of aircraft engine exhausts. He closed with the silhouetted outline of another aircraft – he had been briefed that there would not be any Allied aircraft in his patrol sector that night.

The young pilot banked his Hurricane, checked that his machine guns were on ready and lit his gun sight. As he did so, the unidentified aircraft turned and set course for France in cloud. Try as he could, he could not overtake or further close with the other aircraft. Somehow, it was keeping the same distance from his pursuing Hurricane. As he flew in pursuit, the

Von Richthofen landing his Fokker Triplane.

Rittmeister Manfred Freiherr von Richthofen, *Pour le Mérite*.

sky cleared of cloud, and he saw the aircraft ahead was painted red, with small black crosses on the wings and fuselage, and had a rounded tail. Suddenly he realised what the aircraft was. It had three wings and was very small: it was a First World War Fokker Drei Decker, in the markings and red colours of Baron Rittmeister Manfred Freiherr von Richthofen, with eighty confirmed victories to his credit. He was killed in action on Sunday 21 April 1918, by ground heavy machine-gun fire from an Australian Lewis gunner, Robert Buie, 53rd Battery.

The young pilot tried to close with the Fokker Triplane, but could not do so! His Hurricane was five times as fast as a 1917 German Fokker, but he could not catch it: it could fly faster. Running into heavy cloud and rain, he lost his view of the Fokker, and when he came into a clear space it was gone.

At base that night, in the company of his fellow pilots, he related to them what had happened; as he talked, the room went quiet. One pilot said, 'I have had the same experience'. Two other pilots said that they had had the same experience, and the young pilot asked what was going on. Looking at each other, his fellow pilots told him that it was Baron Freiherr Manfred von Richthofen, holder of Germany's highest award, the *Pour Le Mérite*, flying his Fokker Drei Decker No. 1425/17 of JG1, who was killed on his last sortie by Australian ground machine-gun fire on 21 April 1918. The name given to him by Allied airmen during the First World War was 'The Red Baron'.

In official German combat histories, there are records of the Red Baron's red-painted, ghostly Fokker, flying with German Luftwaffe aircraft in the Second World War. As they went into a dogfight with Allied fighters, the Red Baron joined in then faded away. Incredibly, legend has it that a ghostly First World War S.E.5a British fighter of 1918 vintage, nicknamed 'Old Willie', joined in with British fighters attacking German bomber aircraft over Britain. The ghostly, ancient First World War aircraft of wood and fabric construction was faster than its 1940 counterparts! It dived into the approaching German bombers with its two .303 inch machine guns firing, causing the German bomber pilots to swerve out of its way. When the British fighter pilots, who witnessed the S.E.5a attacking the German bomber swarm, were debriefed, they gave accurate reports of the colours and markings of the ghostly S.E.5a, including the fact that the pilot was wearing a scarf which was blowing wildly in the slipstream.

Perhaps the aerial Second World War was also being waged in another dimension alongside ours. Royal Air Force Air Chief Marshal Hugh Dowding, the architect and victor of the Battle of Britain, was a Spiritualist, and firmly believed that his dead pilots were still fighting the enemy in another dimension alongside their still-living comrades.

The Ghostly Card-Playing American Aircrews

During the Second World War, RAF Kimbolton, 8 miles south-west of Huntingdon, was host to the 379th Bomber Group of 8th USAAF, flying the mighty B-17G Flying Fortress. Flying on daylight raids over Germany, the 379th took many casualties to its young American aircrews. The raids on the ball-bearing factories at Schweinfurt am Main, 55 miles from Nuremberg, were very costly; 642 of the 8th's aircrews were killed, captured, or wounded in action on one raid of 291 bombers.

Many deaths occurred in England. On an icy cold morning, 23 January 1945, a heavily laden, bombed-up B-17G swung onto QDM 330, the 2,000-yard long main runway at Kimbolton. The two pilots struggled to get the iced-up Fortress into the air, but one engine failed as they were just off the runway, and the bomber crashed onto a barrack block at Over Hill, just under 2 miles from Kimbolton village. All the B-17G aircrew was killed when the heavy bomb load exploded on impact.

On 8 May 1945, the Second World War ended in Europe (VE Day), and Kimbolton airfield was taken over by the RAF as a recruit-training centre when the Americans left. In September 1945, five RAF recruits reported seeing a crashed American B-17 Fortress on Kimbolton airfield, with the American aircrew, wearing their Second World War flying kit, playing cards amid the wreckage. In 1978, the RAF excavated the remains of a wartime B-17 bomber on Kimbolton airfield. There is no information about what, if anything, they found. Locally in Kimbolton, other persons have seen the American aircrew, still playing cards on the site of the old airbase.

The Ghostly USAAF Airmen landing their B-17 Flying Fortress

The Lincolnshire area provided a mass of American air bases in England. They were the nearest to Occupied Europe, and were home airfields for the mighty B-17G Flying Fortresses who bombed Germany by day. At such a base in Lincolnshire, the ground crews were waiting the return of their squadrons from a bombing raid on Germany when the engine noise of a B-17 was heard in the circuit. As the ground staff watched, they saw red verey lights being fired to signify that they had wounded airmen among the ten man crew of the Flying Fortress. The Fortress touched down smoothly, and rolled down the long runway to lose speed, then turned off onto the perimeter track to its own hardstanding. The ground crew heard the sound of the aircraft's brakes being applied as it reached its hardstanding, and it came to a rocking halt. The cockpit throttles were eased back, and the propellers slowed to a halt. The medics rushed to the rear fuselage hatch, and clambered in ready to administer medical aid. All the ten aircrew were at their stations. Not one moved; they were all dead. All were cold, and had been dead for some time.

How did an aircraft like the massive Flying Fortress manage to fly back from Germany with a dead crew, land, and taxi, and switch off the engines at their hardstanding? All the crew were dead from enemy fire over Germany. All the four petrol tanks for the four engines were bone dry. Who had fired the red verey lights? As the last of the ten dead airmen were carried out of the aircraft, it burst into flames as though doused in petrol – but there was no petrol in its tanks. (Courtesy of Martin Caiden)

The Ghostly USAF Airmen – still with their B-29 Flying Fortress

John Hulme, an ex-RAF aircrew engineer, informs the author that an USAF Boeing B-29 Flying Fortress, one of the host that returned to Britain in 1948 to counter the Russian threat of atomic war, crashed 1,600 feet up

Wreckage of a B-29 Superfortress haunted by the ghost of an airman in flying kit, Bleaklow, Derbyshire.

on the Derbyshire Moors at Bleaklow, in 1948, killing all thirteen aircrew on board.

Dr David Clarke, the well-known author on matters supernatural, informs me that a fellow historian, Gerald Scarratt, had found what he thought was a tiny washer in the wreckage of the B-29, which after cleaning was examined and found to be a gold ring, with a an inscription 'Langdon P. Tanner' thereon. The USAF pilot of the B-29 was Captain Langdon P. Tanner. Gerald Scarratt took a group of aircraft enthusiasts to the B-29 crash site; he bent down to show them where he had found the ring, and when he looked up found the group had ran some ten to fifteen yards away! He saw they were ashen faced, and said that they had seen someone in full flying kit behind him, looking down at he was doing. He told them he had seen nothing, but they said, 'We've all seen him, thanks for taking us up, but we are going'.

Another friend of Dr Clarke, a Mr Ron Collier, was told by a local nurse that when she and her friends were using an Ouija board, the board had spelled out a message 'Where we are now, we are not at rest', and then went on to spell out the names of all thirteen aircrew who had died in the B-29 crash. The crew of the Boeing USAF B-29 Superfortress still haunt the twisted wreckage site of their fatal crash, which is marked by a shrine and a plaque.

The Ghostly German Airman at RAF Gatow, Berlin

Gatow airfield began life as a Luftwaffe (German Air Force) training college, but during the Second World War was used as a fighter base in the defence of Berlin. Gatow became the terminus of the British airlift into and out of Berlin.

During the Berlin Airlift (Operation 'Plainfare') in 1948-1949, the author was stationed at No. 1 Parachute Training School, Upper Heyford, Oxfordshire, but was detached to Germany on ground and air duty, flying in Dakotas, which were normally employed on parachute dropping.

The all-up weight of a C-47 Dakota was 27,000 lb (landing maximum), and its centre of gravity was most important. Loading coal, flour, and POM (potato powder) into the aircraft was a difficult task, as brute strength was required. Another snag was converting from Imperial measures to metric. Needless to say, many a Dakota staggered off heavily laden, and difficult to trim and fly. Three Dakotas crashed, killing ten RAF crews; one York crashed, killing five crew; and one Hastings with five crew (one of whom was the co-pilot, Sergeant J. Toal, Glider Pilot Regiment).

RAF Gatow, Berlin, was haunted by the ghost of a very tall German Luftwaffe airman, dressed in a Luftwaffe blue greatcoat with collar rank badges, and *Waffenfarben* (Unit badges) shoulder straps. The same form of greatcoat was worn by all ranks, so unless the ghost is seen by an aviation expert one cannot tell which rank he was, or what unit.

According to German and British witnesses, the Luftwaffe ghost has been seen in various parts of the airfield and buildings, always dressed in a German Luftwaffe-issue greatcoat, and disappearing into thin air after a few minutes. It is said that the ghost is German, but it could be one of the airmen who died during the Airlift.

Avro Lincoln B.I RF 398

Avro Lincoln B.I, Serial number RF 398, was built to Air Ministry Order Specification B.14/43 by Armstrong Whitworth Aircraft Company, and designed to replace the famous Lancaster in RAF Bomber Command. Too late to see combat in the Second World War, the Lincoln did see active service in post-war RAF operations against terrorists in Malaya and Kenya. In total, 528 Lincolns were built, with the last operational Lincolns being withdrawn in 1963.

Lincoln RF 398 rotted on an airfield for nearly thirty years, until the RAF decided to put the old bomber in the Museum hangar at RAF Cosford, Shropshire.

It took some eleven years for the old Lincoln to be restored by RAF Apprentices at RAF Cosford, with the aircraft locked each night in the hangar. The nightly RAF Camp Patrol passing by the hangar began to hear strange noises coming from inside: ground crew voices were heard, radio static, engines running up and machine guns being fired (the sound of machine guns being fired is strange – all machine gun testing is done on the rifle and machine gun butts, outside and separate from other buildings). All as though it was a normal RAF 2nd Line servicing hanger in full blast of work.

One of the Camp Patrol unlocked a small side door, and investigated. The sounds appeared to come from RF 398, but on examination there was no one in the Lincoln, or in the hangar. The ghostly noises were reported to the authorities, who carried out an investigation.

Enquiries revealed that personnel who had worked on the restoration found that the interior of RF 398 was always warm, with temperatures in the 70s even thought it was below freezing outside and inside the hangar. All other aircraft in the hangar were freezing cold. With the hangar doors open, the other aircraft in the hangar were covered in dust, but not RF 398; its fuselage was shining black, as though recently washed and polished.

A battery-powered tape recorder was placed in the cockpit of RF 398, and all doors to the hangar were locked. Next day, the recorder was retrieved, and when played back inaudible voices were heard in the empty aircraft in an empty, locked hangar. It was as though the Lincoln was in flight, with crew intercom and R/T in full use between the aircrew and ground airfields.

Several personnel stated that they had seen an airman, clad in Second World War flying clothing, walking through the hangar; mystified by his appearance, they then realised they could see the museum's aircraft through the airman's figure. It was a ghostly airman; why, and who it was, is unknown. Interest being raised on Lincoln RF 398, airmen began to relate stories of having worked on the aircraft for eleven years, and having experienced ghostly voices, the noise of combat radio chatter and of seeing airmen dressed in Second World War flying kit.

Peter Underwood, the famous writer of forty-six books on the supernatural, together with some members of the Ghost Club Society spent a night in the Lincoln bomber. Peter and his wife saw a shadowy figure dressed in Second World War flying clothing walking towards the tail of the old Lincoln. Another member saw the same figure from a different angle. (Courtesy of Peter Underwood)

Ex-RAF Flight Engineer John Hulme, of Holmes Chapel, Cheshire, flew in Lancasters and Lincolns for eight years. He visited RAF Cosford with a lady friend named Meg and two ex-RAF friends, and was allowed to board Lincoln aircraft RF 398 on a nostalgic visit.

He writes as follows: 'We climbed aboard, and what struck me was it seemed small to what I remembered. Once up front I sat in the skipper's seat with Meg in the Flight Engineer's tip-up seat. The cockpit layout of the Lincoln is similar to the Lancaster, and the navigator's table is behind the skipper's seat, with a Terry Anglepoise reading lamp on the map table.

'Meg and the others were chatting for about thirty minutes or so, as I was showing her how to start engines, starboard inner first, pre-flight checks, and so on. Well … here comes the interesting part! It was a very hot summer's day at Cosford, and it was very hot in the hangar indeed. Meg suddenly remarked that how cold it had got, all of a sudden. We three others felt the drop in temperature and one of them said "I think we could be in for a happening!" Temperature drops are common in paranormal situations! The next thing was the sound of a squelch from the back of my position in the driving seat. We all looked round and saw the Terry lamp on the navigator's table moving on its hinge up and down; then, with the lamp pointing at Meg it flashed on, and then off! At this point Meg felt the presence of another someone coming up from the bomb aimer's position in the nose; a very friendly someone or something! Then the temperature started to rise again.

'The strange thing was that all electrics in the Lincoln were disconnected, and I then inspected the fuse panel; there were no fuses fitted! The lamp had no electric power, so how did it flash on and off? One of the other chaps with us said that it must have happened because we had a woman aboard. This was of course unusual; then, women did not fly in Lincolns.

'When Meg was asked if she had felt frightened, she said "no – it was very friendly presence."

'So, there you have it! Another of the strange things that was supposed to happen round this old Avro Lincoln aircraft in the Cosford hangar.'

The RAF Middleton St George Ghost

RAF Middleton St George, 5 miles east of Darlington, Durham, opened as a three-tarmac runway bomber airfield on 15 June 1941, as a permanent base. Five hangars were built: one B type, one C type, one J type, and one T type. All had offices built on the sides to accommodate various admin, operations, and engineering staff and stores.

Eleven Canadian and British squadrons were based on the airfield until the Ministry of Defence sold it in 1964. It later became Teesside Airport, and the Officers' Mess became the St George airport hotel. The five hangars were kept.

During the winter of 1959, when the RAF was still in occupation, an RAF CTO (Chief Technical Officer – Engineering) was working late, checking RAF Form 700s for work carried out during the day on aircraft (Form 700 is a vital piece of paper. It has to be signed by every airman who works on an aircraft before the aircraft is handed over to the pilot. If there is a signature missing, the pilot will not accept the aircraft).

As the officer sat in his office in No. 1 hangar, he became aware of someone else in the room. Looking around, he saw the figure of an officer pilot in full Second World War flying kit by a wall. Startled, the CTO spoke to the pilot, who did not reply but vanished through the brick wall of the office. It would appear that the ghostly Second World War pilot was still checking Form 700s!

In 1965 the ghost was seen again in Number Four hangar, this time walking through the side of the hangar. Perhaps he does not know that the Royal Air Force has gone, and the airfield is now for civil aviation use only.

A Ghostly Airman's Icy Hand

RAF Boscombe Down, 1 mile east of Amesbury, Wiltshire, first saw service in 1917 as an RFC grass airfield. During the first few days of the Second World War it saw service with two squadrons of Fairey Battles, but developed into Aeroplane & Armament Experimental Establishment, and later the Empire Test Pilots' School.

The Luftwaffe took great interest in what was being done at Boscombe Down, and took several reconnaissance photographs from a great height (the author has several of them in his collection). However, the base only had five small air raids during the war.

In the Forties, when the author was stationed at nearby RAF Netheravon, one of his jobs was to drive to Boscombe Down and get the daily meteorological report. He was always asked to stay for a cuppa and a chat, and picked up what was happening at the base.

Regretfully, there were many crashes at Boscombe Down. One of the worst was when an experimental Lancaster bomber collided with an Airspeed Oxford while both were on a left-hand landing and take off circuit above the airfield.

In 1947, during a chat, the author was told that a ghost haunted Airmen's Billet 19. It appeared that an airman, billeted in Billet 19, had asked to be taken up for a 'Gash Flip' (passenger ride in an aircraft), but the aircraft crashed, and all on board were killed instantly. The night after the fatal crash, an oppo (friend) of the dead airman was awakened by the feeling of an icy cold hand gripping his neck. Scared to death, he jumped out of bed and saw, glimmering over the dead airmen's bed, a transparent bluish light, and heard the dead airmen's voice saying, 'I want my kit.'

The airman's ghost kept appearing in Billet 19, to the consternation of the powers that be. To solve the problem, the Billet was locked and unused for over a year.

Since 1947, the author has visited and dined in the Officers' Mess, Boscombe Down, frequently, as several relatives and friends work there. He asked if there still was a ghost, but no one had reported one. RAF accommodation H Blocks were built in the fifties on the site of Billet 19.

The RAF Mildenhall Ghosts

RAF Mildenhall, 12 miles north of Bury St Edmunds, Suffolk, opened in 1934 as a 3 Group Bomber airfield, one of a great many planned for the defence of England against the German Luftwaffe.

One of the future squadrons destined to serve at Mildenhall were No. 149 Squadron, formed on 3 March 1918, and equipped with F.E.2b biplane aircraft intended to be used as night bombers. The F.E.2b was one of the best fighters produced for the Air Force during the 1914-1919 war, and No. 149 Squadron carried out night bombing attacks on German bases in occupied Belgium and northern France with great success.

On 12 April 1937, No. 149 Squadron moved into Mildenhall equipped with Vickers Wellington Mark I twin-engined bombers (Second World War nickname 'Wimpey'). The Second World War aerial war began slowly after 3 September 1939, with desultory action by both the Royal Air Force and the recently formed German Luftwaffe. No. 149 Squadron began to use its Wellingtons on day raids on the German Fleet and its harbours, and was the first squadron so to do.

On 18 December 1939, nine Wellingtons of 149 Squadron took off during daylight hours in a raid on Germany, intending to return under the protective cover of darkness. Two Wellingtons had to abort their mission due to engine trouble, which left seven heading for Germany. At 5.00 p.m., the Wellingtons began to return and land alongside the paraffin gooseneck flare-marked runway. Three landed safely in the gloom of night, but four were missing. At 5.30, the waiting ground staff heard the sound of a single aircraft engine; Wellingtons had twin engines, and one mechanic was heard to say, 'That ain't no Wimpey!' In the light of the flickering gooseneck flares, the watching ground crew saw the incredible sight of a First World War F.E.2b biplane coming in over the airfield. The leather-helmeted pilot was clearly visible, as were his flying goggles and scarf. The

No. 149 Squadron walking out to their Wellingtons, Mildenhall, 1941.

First World War F.E.2b

watching ground staff saw a gloved hand reach out of the F.E.2b's cockpit and throw something out; as he did so, the biplane increased speed, and flew low and fast out of sight. The mechanics on the ground rushed to see what had been thrown out of the cockpit, and found a metal spanner with a hand-written note attached. The Duty Officer took the note. It read, 'Wellington aircraft No. N2961, Squadron Code letters OJ-P, is down in the North Sea'.

Later, it was established that the Wellington N2961 had ditched in the sea, 40 miles off land; all the crew perished. The pilot of the ghostly FE.2B had informed the Duty Officer that one of 149 Squadron's aircraft was lost. The ghostly F.E.2B must have been flying with the Wellington N2961 when it ditched.

The RAF Marston Moor Ghost

RAF Marston Moor, 8½ miles west of York, opened in 1941 as a Bomber airfield of 7 Group. The airfield was used for aircrew conversion to bomber from other types of aircraft. As a training unit, it had its quota of aircraft crashes, some of them fatal.

The Commanding Officer of RAF Marston Moor, from April to September 1943, was Group Captain G. L. Cheshire, VC, DSO, and two

Group Captain Geoffrey Leonard Cheshire, VC, DSO and two bars, DFC.
(*Chaz Bowyer*)

Bars, and DFC, who later wrote of his experiences at the airfield. He told of one day, when a training aircraft caught fire in the air, and was struggling to make it back to Marston Moor in spite of the aircrew being told to bale out. The pilot of the stricken aircraft decided to crash land on the airfield, as it was the best chance of survival and would not endanger innocent people on the ground. The aircraft crashed on the airfield, and Group Captain Cheshire was on the scene at once with the Airfield Crash tender and ambulances. He went into the tangled wreckage, some of which was on fire, and saw a man in the midst of the carnage. Cheshire stopped, saw the man was alive, but not apparently in need of assistance, and went to look for the other aircrew that he could help. He found that all the aircrew were dead from the impact of crashing.

The airfield crash team and ambulance removed the seven dead aircrew from the crash site, and Cheshire went to the Station Medical Officer, who had remained at the scene. Cheshire asked who the lone survivor was he had seen in the midst of the wreckage. The Medical Officer replied that there were no survivors; all had perished in the crash. Cheshire told the Medical Officer that there had been a survivor; he had seen him walking alive through the wreckage. The Medical Officer told Cheshire that all had been killed instantly, but that one body had been found in a hedge, well away from the crash site. The airman had died instantly with a broken spinal cord; he could not have walked away from the crash. Group Captain Cheshire had seen and examined a dead airman, whom he had thought was alive.

The author, while serving in the Royal Air Force, had the privilege of meeting Group Captain Cheshire, and found he was a remarkable officer and gentleman. His decorations were well earned – his Victoria Cross when flying a Mark III Lancaster, No. DV385, code letters KC-A, of 617 Squadron, when acting as Master Bomber over Munich, under heavy German anti-aircraft flak.

RAF Appledram Ghosts

Royal Air Force Appledram (or Apuldram as it was once called) opened as an 11 Group Fighter Advanced Landing Ground, situated 1½ miles south of Chichester, West Sussex, in 1943, on 2 June 1944. It was located on the edge of the Chichester Channel.

The grass airfield had two steel mesh Sommerfeld track runways, and the hardstandings used the same steel mesh. Accommodation was in a canvas-tented camp for air and ground crew, near a pond in Appledram Lane.

The first aircraft to use the airfield were rocket- or bomb-carrying Typhoons of three squadrons: Nos 175, 181, and 182. Three Spitfire squadrons followed them: 310, 312, and 313, flown by Czech pilots. Four days later, on 6 June 1944, the D-Day invasion of France began, and all the squadrons were in the fray at once. Casualties occurred.

A Mrs V. M. Watkins lived at Appledram, and worked in the fields by the airstrip. She says that on occasion she felt a presence near her while she was working. She kept looking over her shoulder, but there was no one there.

One night as she lay asleep, she was awakened at one o' clock in the morning, and saw a figure standing at the foot of her bed; he was wearing a Mae West lifejacket, as worn by fighter pilots. Mrs Watkins closed her eyes in shock, and seconds later opened them; the fighter pilot figure had vanished. Mrs Watkins's husband had a brilliant white light come into his bedroom, and he shouted out; his daughter in the next room also screamed in terror at the same time.

With the end of the Second World War, Appledram reverted to agriculture, and part became the Museum of D-Day Aviation, open 11.00 a.m. to 5.00 p.m., Easter until the end of October, yearly.

In the museum brochure, the Curator states that the airfield is gone, but ghosts and memories remain. There have been many sightings of ghosts, mostly during long summer evenings. The museum is well worth a visit.

The West Kirby Ghost

RAF West Kirby, on the Wirral, Merseyside, was a Recruit Training Centre (known as a square bashing camp), where raw RAF recruits were sent to learn drill and other Service skills. In the Forties, the Author, as a regular raw recruit, spent three months square bashing there. After the Second World War ended, RAF West Kirby gradually ran down as such, and was finally closed, and reverted to agriculture. A Memorial was recently erected (and vandalised), and a thriving old comrades association formed by those who had served there.

Recently, John Hulme, a fellow recruit at West Kirby, told the author that a ghost had been seen on the roadway at a bus stop, outside where the camp gates used to be. The ghost was that of an airman dressed in RAF blue uniform, and a greatcoat and blue woollen gloves. RAF Dress regulations used to state that if a greatcoat is worn, so must blue issue woollen gloves. Many local people have seen the airman ghost standing at the bus stop.

John informed me that in 1953, when he was at West Kirby square bashing, a young airman recruit hanged himself from the camp water

All that remains of RAF West Kirby – a memorial by the road where a ghostly RAF airman was seen.

tower, using his kit bag rope. A case of victimisation by a drill instructor (DI) was reputed to be the cause of the suicide. John says it is possible that the forlorn ghostly airman at the bus stop may be the self-hanged airman's spirit, waiting for a bus to get away from West Kirby, and, perhaps, his torment.

The Ghostly Second World War Bomber

RAF Church Broughton, Derbyshire, was opened in 1942 as a 93rd Bomber Group three-tarmac runway airfield, and closed three years later in 1945 when the Second World War ended. Like many others who had flown from the airfield, nostalgia brings aircrew back to their old haunts! One ex-pilot and his son, together with their two dogs, were walking across the former airfield when they saw a Second World War twin-engined bomber flying very low over the tree tops at the far side of the airfield, then drop to fly at speed a few feet over the ground towards them. The two became aware that the twin-engined bomber was not making any sound as it flew past them, then raced towards the horizon soundlessly, and out of sight. The two dogs started to howl and bark as the soundless aircraft flew over them. The dogs were not on a lead, and raced howling off the airfield. Their owner found them later, shaking and shivering.

Locations of Haunted Armed Forces Airfields and Other Sites

The following airfields and sites are mainly of Second World War usage; some are now civil airfields; some have returned to agriculture. During the Second World War, 70,000 young airmen and women died sudden deaths, and it is not surprising that their spirits return to their airfields. The Ministry of Defence denies that they exist, but to me the volume of evidence is overwhelming, and counters this establishment view. Researchers have been given approximate details of locations.

RAF Appledram: Fighter Command 11 Group. 1½ miles south of Chichester. Ghosts of fighter pilots and aircraft near the Museum. Airfield was an Advanced Landing Ground. Present use agriculture.

RAF Biggin Hill: Fighter Command 11 Group. 5½ miles south-east of Bromley, Kent. Ghostly flying Spitfire and ghostly music. Fighter pilot ghost in Officers' Mess.

RAF Binbrook: Bomber Command 1 Group. 9 miles south west of Grimsby. Haunted Armoury and ghostly airmen. Still in use as an airfield.

RAF Bircham Newton: Coastal Command 16 Group 8 miles north-west of Fakenham, Norfolk. Ghosts in squash court. Now in civilian usage.

RAF Bletchley: Second World War hospital and code-breaking unit. South-east of Milton Keynes. Ghostly nurse in what was the hospital. Now in effect a Second World War museum.

RAF Boscombe Down: Flying Training Command 23 Group, Amesbury, Wiltshire. Ghost of airman was in billet 19. Still in use as RAF airfield.

RAF Bourn: Bomber Command 8 Group. 7 miles west of Cambridge. Ghostly music by a Major Glen Miller orchestra. Now in agriculture usage.

RAF Broughton: Second World War airfield with reported ghostly twin-engined bomber, 9 miles west of Derby.

RAF Cardington: Airship hangar. Ghosts of the crew of crashed airship R101. Bedfordshire.

RAF Colerne: Fighter Command 10 Group. Ghost in old Officers' Married Quarters. 6 miles north-north-east of Bath – in Wiltshire.

RAF Cosford: Technical Training Command 24 Group. 8 miles north-west of Wolverhampton. Haunted Avro Lincoln in hangar.

RAF Coleby Grange: Technical Training Command 27 Group. 6 miles south of Lincoln. Reputed haunted Control Tower.

RAF Church Broughton: Bomber Command 93 Group. 9 miles west of Derby. Ghostly Second World War aircraft flying silently over airfield.

RAF Croydon: Fighter Command 11 Group. German and British ghostly aircrew seen on site 2½ miles from Croydon, Surrey.

RAF Drem: Fighter Command 13 Group. 4 miles north-west of Haddington. East Lothian, Scotland. Ghostly airfield seen out of time.

RAF East Kirby: Bomber Command 5 Group. 4 miles south-west of Spilsby, Lincolnshire. Control tower haunted by USAAF airman whose aircraft crashed on airfield.

RAF Gatow (Berlin): Haunted by the ghost of a Second World War German Air Force officer.

RAF Hawkinge: Fighter Command 11 Group. 2 miles north of Folkestone, Kent. Sound of a Second World War German V1 flying bomb flying.

RAF Helmswell: Bomber Command 1 Group. 7 miles east of Gainsborough, Lincolnshire. Ghostly Second World War music and ghostly aircraft; ghostly airfield lights.

RAF Hendon: Transport Command 116 Group. Now RAF Museum, Hendon. Second World War ghostly airman pilot in flying clothing from a crashed Spitfire there.

RAF Henlow: Maintenance Command 43 Group. 5½ miles north of Hitchin, Bedfordshire. Airman died when his parachute failed to open, and his ghost still screams in terror as he falls.

RAF Hibaldstow: Fighter Command 12 Group. 3 miles south-west of Brigg, Lincolnshire. Ghostly Spitfire lands and then disappears.

RAF Holmesly South: Transport Command 116 and 38 Groups. 6 miles north-east of Christchurch, Hampshire. Sounds of ghostly aircraft taking off and landing; airmen talking and Second World War music playing.

RAF Honington: USAAF 8th Air Force 364 Fighter Group. 7 miles north-east of Bury St Edmunds, Suffolk. A ghostly fighter pilot walks near the spot where he fell to his death from his crashing aircraft during the Second World War.

RAF Kelstern: Bomber Command 1 Group. 5 miles north-west of Lough, Lincolnshire. Sound of ghostly, unseen Rolls Royce Merlin aircraft engines running. Ghostly airman with kitbag bearing one blue band hitching car lifts in area.

RAF Kenley: Fighter Command 11 Group. 4 miles south of Croydon, Surrey. A ghostly Spitfire comes in to land then bursts into flames.

RAF Kimbolton: USAAF 8th Air Force 379 Bomber Group. 8 miles west of Huntingdon, Huntingdonshire. Ghostly American airmen play cards amidst the crashed ruins of their B17.

RAF Lichfield: Bomber Command 93 Group. 3 miles north-east of Lichfield, Staffordshire. Headless airman dressed in Irvin jacket walks the end of Runway 260.

RAF Lindholme: Bomber Command 7 Group. 7 miles north-east of Doncaster, Yorkshire. The most haunted airfield in England.

RAF Linton on Ouse: Bomber Command 6th RCAF Group. 9 miles north-west of York. The Control Tower is, or was, haunted by a ghostly young airman dressed in flying clothing.

RAF Lisset: Bomber Command 4 Group. 6 miles south-west of Bridlington. The 'Grim Reaper' legend airfield. See text.

RAF Marston Moor: Bomber Command 7 Group. 8½ miles east of York. A dead airman walks away from an aircraft crash site though dead.

RAF Middleton St George: Bomber Command 6th RCAF Group. 5 miles east of Darlington, Durham. Aircrew ghost in No. 1 hangar office.

RAF Mildenhall: Bomber Command 3 Group. 12 miles north-west of Bury St Edmunds. First World War F.E.2b seen flying at airfield during Second World War.

RAF Montrose: Flying Training Command 21 Group. 1 mile north of Montrose, Scotland. One of the most famous ghostly airmen, and aircraft hauntings.

RAF North Weald: Fighter Command 11 Group. 2½ miles north-east of Epping Forest, Essex. A dead aircrew pilot haunts the spot where he died using a telephone.

RAF Netheravon: Transport Command 38 Group. Billets still standing where author saw a First World War ghost. Wiltshire – 10 miles north of Salisbury. Now an army camp and parachute club.

RAF Ouston: Wartime 12 Fighter Group airfield. Sick Bay was haunted. 11 miles north of Newcastle.

RAF Scampton: Bomber Command 1 Group. 5½ miles north of Lincoln, Lincolnshire. 617 Squadron Base. Guy Gibson's ghost and that of his dog 'Nigger'.

RAF Stanton Harcourt: Bomber Command 91 Group. 5½ miles west of Oxford. Ghostly aircrew haunt the Control Tower.

RAF Strubby: Bomber Command 5 Group. 3½ miles north of Alford, Lincolnshire. Ghost of a headless airman in hangar.

RAF Wellesbourne Mountford: Bomber Command 91 Group. 5 miles east of Stratford on Avon. Haunted by the ghost of a Second World War Aircrewman.

RAF West Kirby: Recruit Training Centre, The Wirral, Liverpool. Ghost of young RAF recruit by bus stop where Centre was. Memorial at site of former camp gate.

RAF Wickenby: Bomber Command 1 Group. 9½ miles north-east of Lincoln, Lincolnshire. Dead oppo (RAF friend) seen after death by Michael Bentine, comedian serving in the RAF during the Second World War.

Acknowledgements

Acknowledgements and many thanks to:

Air Britain Historians: James J. Halley, author of many books on aviation and a good friend.

David James Atfield: Friend who told me a personal Roman soldier ghost story in 1953.

Dennis Bardens: A premier ghost hunter and author. Sadly, passed away 2006 but well remembered for his splendid books on ghosts and haunting.

Raymond Lamont Brown, author: For his book *Phantoms of the Sea*, and his help in this book.

'Jersey' Cavey: Oppo in the RAF, for information on Jersey ghosts.

Dr David Clarke, author: For his help in research and usage.

Martin Caiden, author: For help and usage on American and other ghosts. Sadly now passed away.

Cornwall County Council: David Thomas, Archivist, thank you for your help on Cernow!

Dayfield Graphics, 1 Concorde Park, Amy Johnson Way, Clifton Moor, York: For photographic CD of York. Thank you chaps! And ladies!

Dorset Tourism, Dorchester, Dorset: Lara Nixey and Mark Simons for help in Dorset Ghosts locations.

Essex County Council: Elli Constantatou, Tourism Officer. For photographs and help.

Exeter City Council: Debbie Lewis and the Council. Many thanks to you all.

Freundesk Traditions Unterseeboote, Cuxhaven, Germany.

The Highland Council Inverness: *Tapadh leat* to Gordan Ireland, Tourism Officer

John Hulme: Author and RAF Aircrew Engineer. A fellow West Kirby Old Boy!

Bryn Jones: Tourism Manager, Salisbury and Stonehenge Tourism, Salisbury Wiltshire. For photographs supplied.

Lynette: Visit Kent Ltd, Canterbury, Kent.

Jak P. Mallmann Showell, Deutches U-Boote Museum, Cuxhaven, Germany.

Alana Michael, Tourism Officer, Gloucester County Council: For photographs. Much appreciated Alana.

Rachel Mildon, Tourism Officer, Devon County Council: For photographs. Much appreciated, Rachel.

Oxford City Council, Town Hall, St Aldate's, Oxford: For photographs supplied.

Peter Sharpe: Author of *U-Boat Fact and Fiction*.

Michelle Slade: Author and Publicity Manager, Wiltshire County Council.

Peter Underwood, master author of forty-six books on the occult: For his help and usage.

United States Naval Historical Center, Washington: For information on Captain Madero and the Thresher Submarine.

United States Of America Embassy Staff, Grosvenor Square London.

RAF HQ Staff, RAF Cardington 1947: For information on the R 101.

RAF Ground Crew, RAF Fayid 1952: For information on North Africa.

RAF West Kirby Association Members.

Somerset County Council: David Bromwich, for photographs supplied.

Tank Museum, Bovington, Dorset: Mrs Janis Tait for the Tiger photograph supplied and information re Tiger 1. Much appreciated.

Wareham Museum Curator Mike O'Hara: For his mass of knowledge and photographs supplied.

Mr and Mrs V. M. Watkins: For information on the Appledram ghosts.

And: My entire world-wide legion of friends and Armed Forces oppos, over the last fifty-five years, with their reports, tales, and stories of the occult. I cannot remember all their names, but remember their accounts. Especially those from the British Isles.

Bibliography and Recommended Further Reading

Barden, Dennis *Ghosts and Hauntings*. Senate, 1965

Belanger, Jeff *Encyclopaedia of Haunted Places*. New Page Books, 2005

Blundell, Nigel and Roger Boar *The World's Greatest Ghosts*. Octopus, 1983

Blundell, Nigel and Alan Hall *Marvels and Mysteries of the Unexplained*. Macdonald and Co., 1988

Caidin, Martin *Ghosts of the Air*. Bantam, 1991

Clarke, Dr David *Supernatural Peak District*. Hale, 2000

Coxe, Antony D. Hippisley *Haunted Britain*. Book Club Associates, 1973

Collman, M. *Hants & Dorset Legends and Folklore*. Pike Ltd, 1975

Currie, Jack *Echoes in the Air*. Crecy Publishing, 2000

Desmond, Kevin *Aviation Ghosts*. Pen & Sword Books, 1998

Exploring the Unknown. Reader's Digest, 1999

Fuller, John G. *The Airmen Who Would Not Die*. Souvenir Press, 1979

Guiley, Rosemary Ellen *Ghosts & Spirits*. Checkmark Books, 1992

Hayes, Anthony *True Ghost Stories From WW1 and WW2*. Bounty Books, 2007

Jones, Richard *Haunted Britain and Ireland*. New Holland, 2003

Lamont-Brown, Raymond *Phantoms of the Sea*. Patrick Stephens, 1972

Legg, Rodney, Collier, Mary and Perrot, Tom *Ghosts of Devon, Dorset, and Somerset*. DPC, 1974

MacDougall, Phillip *Phantoms of the High Seas*. Reed, 1991

Marsden, Simon *The Haunted Realm*. Book Club Associates, 1984

Mitchell, John V. *Ghosts of an Ancient City*. Cerialis Press, 1974

Moss, Peter *Ghosts over Britain*. Book Club Associates, 1977

Puttick, Betty *Supernatural England*. Countryside Books, 2002

Townshend, Marchioness and Ffoulkes, Maude *True Ghost Stories*. Senate, 1995

Underwood, Peter *A to Z of British Ghosts*. Chancellor Press, 1992

Underwood, Peter *Ghosts and Haunted Places*. Piatkus Publishers, 1996

Underwood, Peter *Gazetteer of British, Scottish, and Irish Ghosts*. Souvenir, 1971

Swinton, Sir Ernest *Battlefields of 1914-18*. Newnes Publishers, 1928

List of Haunted Locations in the United Kingdom

ABERDEENSHIRE, SCOTLAND
Braemar: ghost of Redcoat Sergeant Davis seen at Dubhrach.
Gight Castle, Methlick: a ghostly piper plays laments.

ANGUS, SCOTLAND
Montrose Airfield: ghosts of dead airmen, 1913 onwards. B.E.2 seen 1963.

AYRSHIRE, SCOTLAND
Castle Hill, Ardrossan: haunted by the patriot Sir William Wallace, whose giant ghost has been seen on stormy nights in the castle ruins.

ARGYLLSHIRE, SCOTLAND
Ballachulish House: reputed to have the ghost of a clansman in Stuart tartan delivering the news of the Massacre of Glencoe in 1692. After the Massacre, ghostly pipers led the murderers away to be lost in the mountains.
Barcaldine House, Glen Ure: has the ghost of a clan member who was hanged at Ballachulish for a murder he did not commit. Colin Campbell was murdered in 1756, and his ghost walks the scene of his death.
Cortachy Castle, on the River South Esk: has the ghost of two treacherous drummers who were thrown from the ramparts.
Duntrune Castle, Loch Crinan: has a ghostly piper playing in the tower.
Dunstaffnage Castle: haunted by the ghost of Flora MacDonald, the rescuer of Bonnie Prince Charlie.
Glen Shira, Inverary: ghostly Redcoat army marches through the Glen.
Inverary, by Loch Fyne: ghostly galley appears on loch then travels overland.
Inverawe Castle: haunted by the ghost of Duncan Campbell.

AVON
Bath Abbey: has a ghost of a soldier in the stone of a pillar.

BEDFORDSHIRE
Cardington: home of the airship R101 that crashed in flames in France in
    1930. Pilot Irwin called Cardington switchboard after death.
RAF Henlow: haunted by the ghost of an airman who died when his
    parachute failed to open.
Someries House: reputed to be the haunt of a headless ghost, Lord John
    Wenlock, beheaded during the battle of Tewkesbury in 1471.
Woburn Abbey summerhouse: believed haunted by famous pilot known
    as The Flying Duchess. A great lady, who died in aircraft crash, 1937.

BERKSHIRE
Faringdon House: ghost of Sir Robert Pye haunts Faringdon Church, as
    does naval officer Hampden Pye, who was murdered by his wife's lover.
Windsor Castle: the Curfew Tower has ghosts of prisoners' footsteps
    sounding on the stairs. Ghost of King George III haunts room
    overlooking Parade ground and Royal Library.
Windsor Great Park: ghostly sentries on Long Walk beat.

BUCKINGHAMSHIRE
Claydon House, Middle Clayton: Sir Edmund Verney died in the battle
    of Edgehill. His ghost is said to haunt his old house, looking for his
    severed hand.
RAF Bletchley: haunted by the ghost of a green-apron-clad nurse pushing
    a surgical instruments trolley during the hours of darkness.

CARMARTHENSHIRE, WALES
Brecon Beacons: ghostly Wellington bomber flies silently.

CAMBRIDGESHIRE
Cambridge Military Hospital: nursing sister ghost in Ward 13.
Conington, Peterborough, level crossing: ghosts of Second World War
    German prisoners and a ghostly motorcar.
Ex-RAF Bourn airfield: has the sounds of Second World War airmen
    singing Glen Miller songs.

CORNWALL
Blanchminister Castle, Stratton: haunted by the ghost of a crusader knight
    named Ranulph. Nearby is the site of the Civil War site of Stratton
    where 300 soldiers died; their ghosts haunt the site.

Dozmary Pool, Bodmin Moor: haunted by the ghost of evil Jan Tregagle, murderer. (Sir Bedivere threw King Arthur's sword Excalibur into this pool)

Forrabury: ghostly bells under the sea.

Goonhilly Downs: ghostly lugger with full sails set seen in Croft Pascoe Poole.

Mousehole: Merlin's Prophecy.

St Ives Head: ghostly schooner seen in distress then disappears.

St Levan: ghost ship sails from the sea, then overland before disappearing.

Penzance: the Dolphin Inn – ghostly sea captain dressed in a tricorne hat and lace ruffles.

Porthcurno, Land's End: ghostly, fully-rigged sailing ship sails into harbour against the wind then disappears.

Porthgarra, Land's End: ghost of lovers Nancy and William on rocks.

CHANNEL ISLANDS

Jersey: ghosts of the Second World War during wartime German rule.

CHESHIRE

Chester: River Dee, ghost of HMS *Asp*. Also at Pembroke Dock, Wales.

Lyme Park House, Disley: the ghost of Blanche, sweetheart of Sir Piers Leigh who fought and died at Agincourt; she follows his ghostly cortege through the grounds of the house.

Marple Hall: haunted by the ghost of Charles I.

CUMBERLAND

Souter Fell: ghostly Jacobite army marching over the Fell near Mungrisdale.

DERBYSHIRE

Bleaklow, Derbyshire Moors: has the wreckage of a Boeing B29 Superfortress, which is haunted by its crew.

Derwent Valley, Derwent dam: used by Dambusters, 617 RAF Squadron, for training. Ghostly Lancaster seen and heard flying over the dam.

Ex-RAF Church Broughton: silent ghostly aircraft flies over old airfield.

Peak District, Brough: Roman soldiers marching. Near Bradwell and Melandra. Also between Hope and Glossop and the Snake Pass.

Upper Mayfield, Gallows Tree Lane: haunted by the ghosts of Jacobite soldiers who were hanged there.

DEVON

Axminster: Warlake Hill Ghosts.

Branscombe Village: ghost of a hero soldier killed in action seen by his beloved wife between Bovey Cross and Vicarage Hill.

Buckland Abbey: Drake's Drum. Drake's ghost driving headless horses along Tavistock to Plymouth road at night. Villagers at Coombe Sydenham heard ghostly drum beating in 1939.

Clovelly, North Devon: has Velly farm, where it is said that a ghost haunts the cheese-making room.

Exeter, Colyton Crescent: Press Gang ghosts.

Ghostly Second World War French landing craft seen in distress off south coast of Devon.

Torrington, North Devon: the ghost of a soldier killed in action in 1646 haunts Castle Hill.

Wonson Manor, Gidleigh, Dartmoor: four ghostly Cavaliers played cards with the owner of the Manor, who gambled it away.

DORSET

Badbury Rings, Wimborne: 1,000 Saxons were killed by King Arthur's cavalry. Their ghosts haunt the rings.

Bindon Hill above Lulworth Cove: Roman soldiers and horses march and ride on foggy nights. More Roman Legionnaires haunt Seacombe Valley at Worth Matravers.

Chettle Common, Cranborne Chase: Trumpet-Major Blandford haunts Pimperne Village, Blandford, looking for his hand in Bussey Stool Walk.

Clouds Hill, Bovington: Lawrence of Arabia's ghost at his cottage, and on motorcycle.

Corfe Castle, Swanage: housed captured French knights, where they were left to starve to death. Their cries and moans are said to be heard, and lights are said to illuminate the ruins.

Cranborne, on the A3081: haunted by Bronze Horseman ghost from Bottlebush Down.

Filford Farm, Bowood, Bridport: has the ghost of an old soldier where cheese was stored.

Lyme Regis, Broad Street: has the ghost of Judge Jeffries, around where the Great House once stood.

Maumbury Rings, Dorchester: Roman amphitheatre, scene of Gladiator combat. Also eighteenth-century hangings were carried out, and the ghosts haunt the place of hanging.

Poyntington, Sherborne: has the graves of Royalists slaughtered by Roundheads in 1644. Their ghosts have been seen near their graves at night.

Sherborne Castle: has the ghost of Sir Walter Raleigh walking through the grounds on 28 September, St Michaels Eve. Disappears near a tree known as 'Raleigh's Oak'.

Tank Museum, Bovington: has the ghost of 'Herman the German'.

The Boot Inn, Weymouth: built in 1600, the pub has five ghosts! Cavaliers and Roundheads died in a fight.

Worbarrow bay near Corfe: haunted by Roman Legions on the march there, and on Purbeck Ridgeway.

DUMFRIES, SCOTLAND

Corsock Hill: said to be haunted by a ghostly piper playing the pipes.

County Hotel has the ghost of Bonny Prince Charlie in a room, which is now carpeted in tartan.

Dumfries Friary church is haunted by the ghost of King Robert the Bruce and the Red Comyn.

DURHAM

Ex-RAF airfield, now civil, has the ghost of a Second World War pilot in flying kit in No. 1 hangar.

Neville Castle: has the ghost of King David Bruce.

Neville's Cross: was, in 1346, the graveyard of thousands of Scottish solders slaughtered by English archers. Their ghosts haunt the battlefield.

Stamfordham: ghost of a dead pilot haunted Station Sick Bay, Ouston, former RAF airfield.

ESSEX

Bergholt Friary: misty ghost seen in bedroom.

Canvey Point: has the ghost of a Danish Viking warrior who stalks the mud flats.

Ex-RAF airfield North Weald: ghost of a dead pilot trying to make a telephone call.

Great Leigh: Witch's stone boulder, poltergeist activity.

Woodham Ferrers: has the ghost of a Cavalier who haunts Edwin's Hall. And another Cavalier haunts White Tyrells.

EAST LOTHIAN, SCOTLAND

Drem airfield, Haddington: prevision of later airfield.

FIFE, SCOTLAND

Fordell: the miller poisoned Roundheads billeted at the Mill, and they hanged his apprentice, who now haunts the scene.

Nechtanesmere: ghosts repeat battle of May 685.

GLOUCESTERSHIRE

Littledean Hall, Gloucester: has two ghosts, both Royalists from the Civil
War; also a soldier who was killed in a duel in the grounds.

The ghosts of two Royal Messengers riding white horses haunt Prestbury.
One is from 1471, the other from the English Civil War.

HAMPSHIRE

Alma Lane, Caesar's Camp: soldier messenger murdered in 1815 still runs
in Alma Lane.

Bywater House, Boldre: haunted by the ghost of soldier killed there in
1685.

Middle Wallop: the Pheasant pub is reputed to have ghostly airmen singing
Second World War songs.

Portsmouth: ghost of 'Jack the Painter' at Blockhouse Point. Clarence Pier
Obelisk where John Felton was hung in chains. The King's Bastion has
ghost sailors, all wearing full beards.

Tidworth House: the roads around are haunted by a ghostly soldier
drummer.

Victoria Military Hospital, Netley, Southampton: ghostly nurse in uniform,
perhaps Florence Nightingale.

HEREFORDSHIRE

Goodrich Castle, on the River Wye: two lovers tried to escape from the
besieged castle on horseback, but perished in the River Wye. Their
ghosts haunt the castle.

HERTFORDSHIRE

Chequers Street, St Albans: the site of a battle, now haunted by ghosts of
the dead soldiers.

High Down House, Pirton: haunted by the ghost of a Cavalier Goring.

Salisbury Hall, St Albans: has the ghost of a Cavalier who haunts the
Crown Chamber of the Hall. There is also the ghost of a knight in
armour near the bridge of the moat.

Windmill House, Bishops Stratford: reputed to be haunted by the ghost of
a Militia officer who was shot in the grounds.

HUNTINGDONSHIRE

Ex-RAF airfield, Kimbolton: crashed B-17 Fortress; ghostly crew playing
cards.

INVERNESS

Culloden, Drumossie Moor: ghosts of dead Highlanders haunt the site of the battle in 1746. The ghostly Laird of Culdethel, riding a white horse, has been seen, as has the 'Butcher' Duke of Cumberland.

Culloden House: haunted by Prince Charles Edward Stuart.

Eilean Donan Castle: Spanish soldi er had head blown off in 1719 – haunts castle carrying his head.

Loch Ashie moor: May Day scene of repeated ghostly, silent battle between Scots and Norsemen.

Loch Morar, near Mallaig: haunted by the ghost of Simon Fraser, executed after Culloden.

Rait Castle: ghostly battle in ruined castle; also ghostly woman defender with no hands.

IRELAND

Castle Bernard, County Cork: on 21 June 1921, the IRA burnt down Castle Bernard. Ghostly re-enactment each anniversary.

Croagh, County: ghostly fleet of British warships in the sky over their heads.

Galway Bay: ghostly Norse longboats sailing against the wind.

Kerry, Ferrier Cove: ghosts of Spaniards slaughtered by English soldiers in 1579.

Wilton Castle, Wexford: IRA burnt down the Castle in 1923. The ghost of a Captain Archibald Jacob, who died in a horse fall in 1836, haunts the ruins.

ISLES OF SCILLY

Gilstone Reef: 2,000 sailors drowned in 1701. Admiral Sir Cloudesley Shovell haunts the scene by a monument.

ISLE OF SKYE, SCOTLAND

Cuillin Hills: ghostly kilted Highlanders.

Harta Corrie in Glen Sligachan: scene of a 300-year-ago battle between MacDonalds and MacLeods. Re-enacted again and again.

ISLE OF IONA, INNER HEBRIDES, SCOTLAND

The shore at White Sands on Iona is haunted by Danish Vikings who raided the island in 986. A ghostly fourteen-strong fleet of longships have been seen re enacting the raid.

ISLE OF WIGHT

Lucombe Chine: the ghost of HMS *Eurydice* appears off the coast where she sank with great loss of life.

KENT

Aylesford, Kits Cory House: Megalithic barrow on Blue Bell Hill; burial place of British warrior AD 455.

Biggin Hill Airfield: ghostly Spitfire aircraft at full throttle over airfield. Ghostly aircrew seen walking along Runway 21. On cold night, Second World War songs can be heard from ghostly airmen.

Chatham: Old St Mary's Barracks has the ghost of a crippled goaler sailor in Cumberland Block, Cell 34. Admiral Nelson haunts the old dockyard dressed in naval uniform.

Dover airspace: RAF pilot met ghost of the Red Baron.

Dover Castle: murdered drummer boy marches around the castle, sounding his drum.

Downe Court, Orpington: is said to have a cavalier resident – he appears in photographs taken on the stairs and library.

Faversham: thirteenth-century 'Shipwright's Arms' by River Swale haunted by a nineteenth-century ship's captain.

Goodwin Sands, east of Deal: ghosts of sailing ships and a German U-boat.

Hall Place, Bexley: has the ghost of the Black Prince, who appears as a black figure.

Hawkinge, former RAF airfield: bombed by German V1 flying bomb; local people say they sometimes hear a V1 overhead.

Lympne Castle, Hythe: has the ghost of a Roman soldier who fell to his death. Six Saxon soldier ghosts haunt the castle. At Slaybrook Corner, Hythe, a Roman soldier haunts the scene of an ancient battlefield.

Pegwell Bay, Ebbsfleet: ghosts of Hengist and Horsa fight again and again.

Richborough Castle, Sandwich: old Roman Fort; garrison still march in and out.

Rochester Castle: has the ghost of defender Lady Blanche de Warenne, who was killed in a castle siege by an arrow through her heart.

Smarden: The 'Chequers Inn' haunted by the ghost of a murdered sailor.

LINCOLNSHIRE

A ghostly B-17 Flying Fortress landed at an airbase in Lincolnshire after a raid on Germany. All on board were dead, but it was flown in.

Cammeringham: the ghost of Queen Boadicea is reputed to drive her fearsome war chariot through the street of the village, which is close to the Roman Ermine Street, usually early in the morning.

East Kirby airfield, Spilsby: had a haunted control tower with an American Air Force Officer who was in the crew of a Flying Fortress, which crashed.

Ex-RAF Helmswell, Gainsborough: Second World War music has been heard from the airfield; also aircraft engines being tested.

Hibaldstow, former RAF airfield, has a ghostly Mark IV Spitfire coming in to land with the throttle back and flaring out to land perfectly.

RAF Scampton: ghost of Guy Gibson's dog seen in Officers' Mess and area. Guy Gibson believed to haunt the Lancaster Bar of the Petwood Hotel, Woodhall Spa.

The Black Bull, Welton, pub: reputed to have ghostly airmen singing Second World War songs.

Wickenby, former RAF base: ghost of a friend of Michael Bentine seen.

LANCASHIRE

Maghull, near Liverpool: Highlanders haunt the area, and the sound of fighting is heard; also headless horsemen ride at night.

Newton le Willows: echoes to the ghostly sound of troops walking to be hanged in 1648 by Cromwell.

West Kirby, The Wirral: ghost of a dead airmen outside former RAF Station West Kirby.

LONDON

Apsley House: the home of the Duke of Wellington is said to be a haunt of Cromwell, as is Red Lion Square.

Berkeley Square: haunted house.

Holland House, Westminster: haunted by the ghost of the executed Cavalier Lord Holland.

Kensington Palace: reputed to be haunted by the ghost of King George II.

Knightsbridge, The Grenadier pub: has an officer ghost in the cellar.

National Maritime Museum, Greenwich: the admirals' ghosts.

St Martin's Lane, Coliseum Theatre: haunted by the ghost of a First World War soldier killed in action in France.

Thames Estuary: the ghost of the *Great Eastern* (and at Birkenhead).

Tower of London: haunted by ghost of Sir Walter Raleigh, who appears along Raleigh's Walk by the Bloody Tower. Ghosts have also been seen there by sentries.

Wapping Dock: haunted by the ghost of Captain Kidd.

Wellington Barracks: headless female ghost, wife of Guardsman, seen by sentries.

Westminster Abbey: a ghost soldier appears at the tomb of the Unknown Soldier.

MIDDLESEX

Hendon airfield: ghost of a Spitfire pilot in buildings.

RAF Museum, Hendon: ghost of a dead airman, who crashed into tree in a B.E.2c aircraft of the First World War.

MIDLOTHIAN

Edinburgh Castle: small headless drummer boy drifts through castle.

Edinburgh: Mercat Cross has the ghosts of soldiers who died at the battle of Flodden, 1513.

Grassmarket and West Bow: ghosts of Major Weir and his sister Grizel, both executed for witchcraft in 1670.

MORAYSHIRE, SCOTLAND

Castle Grant: has the ghost of a piper from Culloden battlefield that brought news of the defeat.

Dunphail Castle, Forres: haunted by five headless Highlanders.

NORFOLK

Bircham Newton RAF airfield: ghostly airmen in tennis courts.

Potter Heigham, Hickling Broad: faithful drummer boy still sounds his drum to his lover after his death on the ice-covered broad.

The Old Hall, Ranworth: has the one-time Squire Colonel Thomas Sidney haunting the grounds of the Hall each 31 December.

Wroxham Broad: ghostly Roman soldier appears during March and October, followed by gladiators to the site of Roman Games.

NORTHAMPTONSHIRE

Grafton Regis Manor House: burnt down by Roundheads in 1643, after a battle. During the Second World War, ghosts refought the battle during the night.

Passenham Village: haunted by a seventeenth-century ghostly knight, Sir Robert Banastre, who walks the street in full armour.

NORTHUMBERLAND

Otterburn: scene of battle, 1388; ghostly armies fighting on site, 1960.

ORKNEY, SCOTLAND

Scapa Flow: Drake's Drum was heard on the battleship *Royal Oak* shortly before it was sunk; there is also the ghost of a sailor killed by a Second World War U-boat.

OXFORDSHIRE
Ex-RAF airfield Stanton Harcourt: haunted control tower.
Woodstock Manor, Woodstock: occupied by Cromwell's cronies in 1649.
    A poltergeist created mayhem till all cleared out.

PERTHSHIRE
Aberfeldy, Ballechin House: Major Robert Steuart returns as ghostly black dog.
Belfield House: haunted 1915, during First World War.
Glenshee: ghost of Redcoat Sergeant Davis, murdered in the glen in 1749.
Pass of Killiekrankie haunted by the ghosts of Highlanders and William
    of Orange's troops. Red glow bathes the Pass in the twilight, and the
    ferocious battle erupts again and again.

SHROPSHIRE
Ludlow Castle: Lady Marion de la Bruyere, a defender of the castle, who
    walks up the stairs of the castle. The nearby Globe Hotel is haunted by
    a soldier who died in the castle.
RAF Cosford: has an Avro Lincoln bomber in a hangar, in which ghostly
    events occur.

SOMERSET
Cadbury Camp, near Yeovil: Midsummer's Eve, King Arthur's knights
    emerge and water their horses.
Curry Mallet Manor House, Taunton: has the sounds of unseen hands
    fighting to the death.
Dowsborough: the site of a camp where the ferocious Danes fought each
    other to death when drunk. The sound of fighting and dying can still be
    heard.
Gaulden Manor, Tolland: three bloodstained Cavaliers haunt the chapel
    of the Great Hall; they have been seen standing in front of the panelled
    walls. Cromwell's Roundheads were quartered at the Hall during the
    War.
Glastonbury Abbey: King Arthur's Grave.
Glastonbury: ghostly armoured soldiers have been heard.
Heddon Oak, Crowcombe: was used as a gallows, and has the ghostly
    sounds of men dying by hanging.
Locking Manor: haunted by the ghosts of Sir John Plumley and his wife,
    walking with their dog. He was hanged for supporting Monmouth, and
    his wife committed suicide.
Luttrell's Folly, Conygar Hill, Dunster: the sound of unseen marching men
    heard by two ladies.
Porlock Weir: three sailor ghosts who drowned at sea.

Sedgemoor, Weston Zoyland: the scene of the Battle of Sedgemoor has the ghost of the Duke of Monmouth who, after the battle, was executed in 1685. He has also been seen at the nearby Woodyates Inn.

Taunton: Castle Hotel has the ghost of a soldier who has been seen on the stairs and hallway. The Tudor Inn is said to be prisoners' haunt; Judge Jeffries' Courtroom and Hangman's Walk runs past the Inn.

The Fleur de Lys pub, Norton St Phillip, Frome: the scene of the execution by hanging of chained rebels, and their ghosts still linger there.

The River Cary: is said to have ghosts saying 'Come on over and fight.'

SUFFOLK

Hoxne: the Gold Bridge over the river is haunted; the gleam of King Edmund's golden spurs has been seen in the water on moonlight nights.

RAF Honington airfield: pilot baled out over airfield, but died when he hit a hangar roof; his ghost re-enacts his fall and death.

RAF Mildenhall had a ghostly Wellington bomber lost at sea; F.E.2b First World War aircraft appeared with ditched message.

SURREY

Croydon Airfield: now a housing estate, but Second World War songs being sung by ghostly airmen have been heard. A ghostly German airman has been seen in an old hangar. In one of the estate houses, a ghostly RAF pilot has been seen.

Kenley, the former RAF airfield: a ghostly Spitfire flies and crashes.

Westbrook House, Godalming: reputed to be haunted by the ghost of Bonny Prince Charlie, who walks the gardens.

SUSSEX

Arundel Castle: the castle was bombarded by Cromwell and some locals say they can hear the roar of cannon. The castle library has a ghost known as the Blue Man who reads the library books.

Battle Abbey: haunted by the bloodstained ghost of King Harold, still with the fatal arrow in his eye.

Brede Place, Rye: ghostly monk called father John haunts the area.

Eastbourne, Hurstmonceaux Castle: the ghost of the Giant Drummer who marches round the Drummer's Hall haunts the castle.

Ex-RAF Appledram, Chichester: ghostly pilot seen, and unknown presence felt.

Pevensey Bay: there is a legend that a ghostly army of men, led by William Rufus, marches from the sea to Pevensey Castle moat.

St Nicholas's Churchyard, Brighton: has a grave from which a knight in armour emerges and rides round the churchyard on moonlight nights.

Siddlesham, Chichester: The Crab and Lobster Inn is reputed to have five Cavaliers, who died in a firefight with Cromwell's troops.

Winchelsea, Churchyard: Negro drummer haunts churchyard

Worthing Point: on 17 May, a ghostly sailing ship is lost off the coast with all hands.

STIRLINGSHIRE, SCOTLAND

Barracks of Argyll and Sutherland Highlanders: ghost of sentry heard on battlements.

SUTHERLAND, SCOTLAND

Sandwood bay: a sailor ghost has been seen on beach and cottage near Cape Wrath lighthouse.

WARWICKSHIRE

Edgehill: the Public Record Office regards reports of a re-enactment of the battle of 1642 as authentic.

Shuckburgh Hall, Daventry: has the ghost of a Militia officer who shot himself, as he could not marry the lady of the Hall.

WEST LOTHIAN, SCOTLAND

Blackness Castle, Blackness: the Prison Tower has the ghost of a knight in armour walking the stairs.

The Binns, Blackness: reputed to have the ghost of General Tam Dalyell, who played cards with the Devil.

WESTMORELAND

Lowther Castle: haunted by the ghost of Sir James Lowther, driving a four-in-hand carriage.

WIGTOWNSHIRE, SCOTLAND

Culzean Castle has a ghostly piper of Clan Kennedy, playing the pipes on Piper's Brae (hill).

WILTSHIRE

Bowerchalke Village: ghosts of Roman soldiers haunt Patty's Bottom on one side of village, still fighting the Britons.

Lacock Abbey: haunted by William Longspee, killed on Crusade in 1250.

Longleat House: a ghost reads books in the library.

North Tidworth Army camp: a ghostly Roman soldier carrying a *Gladius* sword has been seen frequently. A ghostly kilted soldier has been seen on the rifle range.

Odstock Hospital, Salisbury: ex-American hospital; ghostly music during night from near Woodford Ward.

RAF Boscombe, Amesbury: had a ghost in Billet 19 which is now believed to be at rest.

RAF Netheravon, Salisbury Plain: ghost of a First World War airman in billet.

Stonehenge Circle, Amesbury, Salisbury Plain: ghostly figure of a drummer boy.

Syrencot House, Brigmerston: has the ghost of a paratrooper in the kitchen.

Wardour Castle, Ansty: ruined, but the nearby lake is haunted by one of the defenders, Lady Blanche Arundell, who was slaughtered with twenty-four other defenders.

YORKSHIRE

Ex-RAF Linton on Ouse: Control Tower haunted by dead RAF hero.

Ex-RAF Lindholme airfield: ghosts of dead airmen.

Ex-RAF Marston Moor airfield, Marston Moor: had an airman who appeared alive but was dead.

Fulford, River Ouse: scene of a fatal duel; the ghost of the loser appears at the site of the duel.

Goodramgate, Holy Trinity Church: headless ghosts have been seen in churchyard.

Long Marston: Battle of Marston Moor, 1644; ghostly Cavaliers seen in Long Marston village. Cromwell is said to haunt the Old Hall in the village.

Tadcaster, Bramham Moor: battlefield in 1408; now a cricket pitch, where at night the sounds of the battle are sometimes heard.

The Mansion House, near the River Ouse: Cavalry ghost in the cellar.

The Micklegate Bar: beheaded Jacobite ghosts haunt the scene of their beheading.

The Treasurer's House, near the Minster: has a troop of Roman soldiers in the cellar.

York Minster: ghost of a naval officer walks inside.

Watton Abbey: has a Cavalier ghost who stands by a fireplace in a bedroom.

List of Haunted Locations Abroad

BELGIUM
Mons: ghostly soldiers on horseback, knights in armour, bowmen, and
glowing angels seen during British retreat, August 1914.

CRETE
Frangocastella: Turkish and Greek troops fought battle, 1828. Battle re-
enacted on 17 May each year.

CROATIA
Varasidin: an aerial army seen, led by warrior with a flaming sword, last
seen August 1888.

FRANCE
Dieppe, Puys: ghosts of failed Allied raid in August 1942.

GERMANY
Boully, Germany: ghosts seen in glass windows.
Gatow airfield, Berlin: ghostly German Luftwaffe officer.
Rodenstein and Schnellert, Germany: the Wild Horde of ghosts, last seen
1764.
Ujest, Silesia, Germany: military ghostly cortege in sky, 1785.

ITALY
Rome: Napoleon's ghost seen in Palazzo.

UNITED STATES OF AMERICA
United States Capitol and White House Ghosts.

Gatlinburg, Tennessee: Civil War ghostly soldiers.

Antietam, Maryland: battlefield; Bloody Lane.

Harper's Ferry, then Virginia: ghost of John Brown.

Gettsyburg, Pennsylvania: battlefield haunted by soldier ghosts.

Chickamauga, Tennessee: soldier ghosts haunt the battlefield at night.

Cedar Creek, Virginia: church on battlefield haunted.

San Pasqual, San Diego County, California: ghostly solders re-enact the battle.

Elmore, Ohio: ghostly American soldier rides a motor cycle, 21 March each year.